A METHOD OF PRAYER

FOR MODERN TIMES

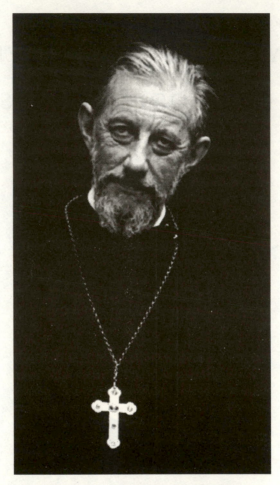

Bishop Jean, Eugraph Kovalevsky,
founder of the French Orthodox Church

A METHOD OF PRAYER

FOR MODERN TIMES

by Eugraph Kovalevsky, Bishop Jean of Saint-Denys, founder of the
French Catholic Orthodox Church
based on a translation of the third French edition
by Esther Williams
edited and updated to conform to the fifth French Edition
by Robin Amis and Raymond Hébert
with the approval of Bishop Germain, successor to Mgr. Jean

Published by

PRAXIS INSTITUTE PRESS

Praxis Institute Press
P.O.Box 375, Newburyport, MA 01950 USA
Tel:(508) 462 0563 Fax:(508) 462 0563

Printed in Great Britain by BPCC Wheatons Ltd., Exeter
Typesetting by Bill Tidwell.
Praxis Research Institute, a non-profit institution dedicated to the recovery of lost or
forgotten Christian teachings, depends on outside funding and voluntary assistance, and
gratefully acknowledges the ongoing contributions of a supporting team of translators,
editors and proofreaders around the world.

International English language edition first published 1993.

British Library Cataloguing-in-Publication data:
A catalogue record for this book is available from the British Library.
Library of Congress catalogue card number:
ISBN 1-872292-08-8-18-6

CONTENTS

PART ONE : THE STEPS TO PRAYER

PART TWO : THE LORD'S PRAYER

PART THREE :
COMMENTARIES BY THE FATHERS

PUBLISHER'S INTRODUCTION

"A truly spiritual life is not possible without prayer — which is spiritual life in action. Prayer is the raising of our mind and heart to God. One may say that to pray means bringing right feelings and attitudes into action."

In this way Russia's Saint Theophan the Recluse (d. 1984) defined prayer.

Later he wrote: *"What is prayer? It is the listening of our mind and heart to God. As soon as any pious feeling starts to move, prayer is there too. To pray seems to bring pious feelings and attitudes into action, leading to a quickening or kindling of life, and forming a spirit of devotion. If a person has no devotion, how can he pray? And if devotion is the life of our spirit, we can understand that only a person who knows how to pray can be said to possess spirit — and that is just how it is."*

Like Theophan's writing, this book by Eugraph Kovalevsky — better known as Bishop Jean of Saint-Denys, Russian founder of the French Catholic Orthodox Church — will seem to many people to look at prayer in quite a new way; yet those who are experienced in the life of prayer will recognise it as being both genuine in its insights and truly fruitful in the practical advice it gives. Again we find that Theophan — also an Orthodox bishop before he became a hermit — links prayer to breathing in a way very similar to that in which Bishop Jean speaks about *breath prayer* or prayer of the breath.

About this, Theophan wrote: *"When we breathe, the lungs expand and draw in the lifegiving elements of the air, and in prayer the depths of the heart are thrown open and the spirit ascends to God to commune with Him and receive the gifts this brings. And just as in breathing the oxygen is received into the blood and then distributed to bring life to the body, so, in prayer, what is received from God enters our innermost being and gives new life to everything there.*

"Prayer is the quickening of the spirit, in a sense its deification. As someone in a myrrh distillery becomes familiar with myrrh, so anyone ascending to God becomes interpenetrated with divinity."

Based on these links with a great past, it would be easy to make many claims for this book. But it is better to say little, yet to substantiate it well, and I believe that these passages from Theophan will not only help to make clear the real value of the book, but will support the claim that it lies in the direct line of that great and ancient tradition of prayer to which Theophan himself so clearly belonged.

Beyond this, we can say certain other things about this book which the heart that is experienced in prayer will, by grace, be able to confirm for itself: that it accurately touches on the problems faced by us when we attempt to live the life of prayer under the conditions of modern life; that it not only acknowledges the existence of the great paradox of prayer — that in which grace depends upon our efforts yet does not respond in any predictable way to our actions — but that it actually provides a practical resolution to the practical problems caused by this antinomy.

Here then is a book with real meaning for those attempting to approach the life of prayer, a compendium of practical solutions to those problems that seem so trivial to men of the world, but which look so large in the world of prayer, a concise primer for those beginners at serious prayer that can yet open out to lay the foundation of a rule of prayer for those who would live the life of prayer in ordinary life.

Here, in a word, is a touch of tradition that, instead of playing over ancient solutions, proves to be well adapted to modern man with all his problems and pressures. Here, in fact, for those who have truly spiritual questions, are some genuinely new, yet truly spiritual answers.

PREFACE
TO THE FRENCH FOURTH EDITION

We can imagine the existence of a man, and that of all men, as a road mapped out in advance yet at the same time unknown. On traveling it, we do not meet other men as if they were the same, present, near, and they too are preoccupied with their own route; all these others, in fact, do not appear on the way as a major interest.

But on this route, we always meet somebody enigmatic and essential. Perhaps the difficulties of the journey preoccupy man to the point of absorbing all his energies and making him almost blind to what is going on around him, but the person in question passes by everyone and always crosses their path.

Who is it that all human beings, without exception, meet on the path of their life?

We know him at the same time as architect and entrepreneur, engineer and sculptor, priest and sacrificer, vintner and merchant, or better, housekeeper, restaurateur and hotelier. You have probably realized by now that this is Wisdom, which fills the universe without imposing itself, and which is the source of meaning of all that is, for it is Wisdom that builds, carries, offers, vivifies and divides up life.

Thus, no technique for growth exist without seeing or receiving it in its measure. This technique is that of prayer, the subject of this book, and it is enough that a man is able to serve, then the benefit is poured out on hundreds. In effect, until he has met Wisdom he walks alone, from then on, as he begins to construct the heart and set it on fire by the activity of prayer, this Wisdom multiplies itself with a phenomenal speed and comes to illuminate and accompany the quest of very many men.

Prayer, which includes meditation, awakening, silence, chanting, bodily and spiritual rhythms, appears to modern man to belong 'amongst the rubbish.' Our times see these experiences and their results through imprac-tical moralizing or as obscure traditions.

To begin is easy, the end is seductive, but how to proceed is agonizing. We can take its measure on the basis of this description, the fruits of the experience of a sage who lived in the shadow of the Spirit, and of the teachings of the Elders.

And at the moment when the reader will become the doer, even if only temporarily and still a little sceptically, he will provoke in himself and among others such a peace that he will assimilate the technique with no more to say.

In the following stage, the one who acts will have come to the age of Wisdom. This is the end of the work, for here one knows, and here one is known.

✝ GERMAIN Bishop of Saint-Denys
and the Orthodox Catholic Church of France

PREFACE
TO THE FRENCH FIFTH EDITION

The vivifying teaching of Bishop Jean on prayer reaches a large audience. A fifth edition has become necessary. Retaining the character of the original text, which was a course of *theory and praxis* given at the Institute Saint-Denys — the Institute of French Orthodoxy in Paris — this edition corrects the contradictions, makes the references more exact, and reinstates the practical questionnaires at the end of each chapter for the personal observations of the reader. This work of adaptation of the text, carried out by Deacon Jean-Francois Var, clearly reveals the strength of soul, the spiritual paternity, and the inspiration of the teacher bishop.

The apostles, asking Christ one day for a prayer, received 'the Prayer', the Lord's Prayer. The best commentary on this prayer is presented at the end of the studies in this small work, and allied with other commentaries by the Fathers. These lights of the Light give meaning and taste to a return towards the paradise which forms the experience of prayer.

✝ GERMAIN Bishop of Saint-Denys
and the Orthodox Catholic Church of France

EDITOR'S INTRODUCTION TO THE FRENCH FIFTH EDITION

The source of this work was a cycle of twenty-one 'lessons' given during the year 1958-59 at the Orthodox theological Institute of Saint-Denys by its Rector, Archpriest Eugraph Kovalevsky, the future Bishop Jean of Saint-Denys, published for the use of students in mimeographed form and titled *Technique of Prayer*. Extracts appeared in several issues of *Cahiers Saint Irénée* in 1959-60. Later, the text was edited and the 'lessons' transformed into chapters, taking the form of a book of the same title published in 1971 by Présence Orthodoxe. A new edition followed in 1979, under the direction of Editions Eugraph, in which the chapters were divided into subsections for easier reading. Then in 1981 Editions Friant prepared a new edition, close to that of 1971, but with important differences: the original division into chapters was not entirely respected: all scriptural and patristic references were removed from the text 'for lighter reading,' as were the five last chapters, the extracts from the commentaries on the Lord's Prayer of Origen, Saint Cyprien of Carthage and Saint Cyril of Jerusalem. The 'exercises' which had previously concluded the first eight chapters and had helped to introduce actual practice of the 'methods' taught in those chapters were also omitted. We should also mention other unofficial duplicated versions. The important thing is to note that, of all these editions and versions, only the first was prepared during the life and under the control of the author (d. 1970).

To establish the present text, we have carefully looked at all the versions, and where they diverge, we have systematically given preference to the original, at the same time as correcting a certain number of errors of transcription and printing which were carried forward from edition to edition.

For the best possible intelligibility of the text we have occasionally corrected the punctuation to fit in with usage which has changed over thirty years. In the same spirit, we have retained the division into subsections. In effect, although these were not part of the original edition, they appear to us to be useful in throwing into relief the structure of the whole and the detail of the work in its different chapters, while making it easier to find things in the table of contents. Throughout, we have not hesitated to revise it where it does not appear to correspond to the internal logic of the chapter under consideration. We have also revised some of the explanatory notes.

At the same time we have reproduced in full the 'exercises' by which the readers may try out the methods taught. To tell the truth, the title *A Method of Prayer* applies only to the *first part* of this book. The *second part* is composed of a theological and spiritual commentary on the Lord's Prayer: the Our Father. That is why practical exercises are only given in the eight chapters of the first part.

In the original edition, the mimeographed course, the author began with the following preliminary notes:

"It is important not to lose from sight that the object of this book is a method which the reader is called upon to put into practice by means of the practical exercises and the questionnaires for self-analysis which follow each chapter.

"So to make this task easier:
1.) We will set out the central idea in each chapter.
2.) We will suggest suitable methods.

"The questionnaires for self-analysis which accompany the practical exercises are not planned to serve like an examination in the academic sense of the word, but more to assist the reader in the spiritual formation of his soul. It is up to the individual to collaborate with God in his own salvation. Nevertheless, if certain aspects of our teaching appear obscure to him or seem particularly difficult to understand, we will be happy to answer his questions. While their incognito will be strictly respected, the answers to these questions will be expressed in ways that help everyone, while being put in general terms.

"This course is basically different from that which preceded it (one on Genesis), and the two which follow it, for its aim is to link personal experience with knowledge.

"The lessons which it contains directly address the soul, while as far as possible separating it from abstract reason. Each of them is followed by 'practical exercises' suggested to the student, and by a 'self-questionnaire.'

"*Our fervent wish is to open the path of prayer to everyone ... as far as they wish to go.*"

Another qualification: this term 'method' must not lead us into expectations. The reader who is attracted to corporeal methods is in danger of being greatly misled: to put it another way, there is no guarantee. In effect, nothing is further from the Christian tradition than to consider and treat the body in isolation and apart, independent of the soul and the spirit which, united to it, form the totality of the human individual. It is the same with all authentic traditions, and much can be said about the propensities of contemporary Westerners to practice a purely corporeal yoga, or one that is psychosomatic in a rigorous sense, disconnected from its traditional spiritual support.

To return to the 'method of prayer' taught in the first part of the work, we will see on page after page that this method is inseparable from a theology and spirituality deeply and intimately nourished by the Scriptures and the Fathers. In the same way, in their turn, the theological commentaries, scriptural and patristic, which form the second and third parts and inspire spiritual counsel, inducing a prayerful pace, construct a 'method of prayer.' In different ways the title proves appropriate to the whole book.

"Our wish," wrote the author in the text quoted above, *"... is to open the path of prayer to everyone ... as far as they wish to go."* We will make another wish: to open in the same way the path of reading the Scriptures, that is to say, of hearing the Word of God: The scriptures that Eugraph, as a priest, then as Bishop Jean, had been forced to feed on daily since early infancy, so that he had totally assimilated them. Thus, he had come, rarely and uniquely, to a precise instructional goal, able to recite a passage 'by the book' — an open book. Most of the time, he quoted from the head — or by heart — sometimes slightly modifying the words, at other times combining two passages. In the course of time this continued through all the apostles and all the Fathers, for example, Saint Paul or Saint Irenaeus of Lyons, not to make a choice among the greatest.

So we hope, if it pleases God, that if this book falls into the hands of readers who are not fully familiar with the Scriptures, that we have clearly described all the references, most of them implied or in the form of allusions, which the author made in carrying out his intention. For this we have applied the following rule: we have placed references to literal quotations from the Old and New Testaments between parentheses; we have relegated to notes all references to passages to which the author has referred without quoting exactly, or where he has quoted while making small changes. We have verified and where necessary corrected all the references given in the previous editions. Quite certainly the reader, if he takes the trouble to turn up these passages in Scripture — as he should if not familiar with them, but no matter, the phenomenon will still act in the same fashion — will make discoveries that will be useful *to him at that exact time.*

Perfection is not the world: nevertheless, at the end of this work we consider that this edition has improved on the previous text, particularly in the accuracy of the text. We have therefore the happiness to express our living recognition to all those who have made our task possible, in particular M. Vincent Tanazacq, who has amiably told us about his personal experiences during 1958-59, and M. Guy Barrandon, who began the work of compiling these editions and has taken responsibility for an essential part of the material manifestation of the work. Also we must not forget Mgr. Germain, successor to Bishop Jean, who has encouraged and blessed this enterprise at each of its steps, and whose advice to us has been most valuable. To all, we give thanks.

The Association Eugraph Kovalevsky

PART ONE
THE STEPS TO PRAYER

CHAPTER ONE

PRAYER IS CONVERSATION WITH GOD

The experience of prayer

Words are always inadequate to express what prayer is: experience alone can bring us close to it.

Our times, unfortunately, do not make it easy to experience prayer. How can we become praying souls in such a restless life as ours? Our number one enemy is lack of time, and we are so agitated that we no longer know how to rest. Even if we go on holiday, it is for swimming, for sunbathing at all costs, for climbing peaks or motoring. Can we stay in one place when a few yards away are four roads inviting us to run to 'scenic spots', to visit Romanesque or Gothic churches, etc., etc.?

Nevertheless, there is a certain asceticism running through our life. It is the fashion to eat little and 'naturally', but do we do this in a spirit of spiritual fasting? Certainly not! The reason for this abstinence is rather a confused Hinduism, or the blundering of one who makes use of fasting in an absurd way, simply because he cannot escape a certain nostalgia for the divine.

All these modern circumstances have made it necessary to change the technique of prayer, as the lessons of the past can no longer be applied. What then will be the method to offer to this nervous man of the 20th century, morbidly nervous, tense, easily thrown into confusion, ceaselessly changing the subject?

To speak with God

Saint John Chrysostom, Gregory of Nyssa, Maximus the Confessor, and a great number of Fathers whom we cannot mention here, all describe prayer as 'conversation with God.'

Communication with an intelligent and good man makes us intelligent and good; conversation with God 'makes us godlike,' says Saint John

Chrysostom. Put simply, conversation with God, one of the most precise, direct, and simple forms of prayer, is not just to think, but to speak to God continually. Let us take an example: we are troubled, invaded by anxiety. Instead of analysing, of asking ourselves: should I do this, or should I act in another way - so that thought is an interior production, a dialogue which often becomes a throng in which rise the voices of the memories and anxieties of the past — instead, let us place all that before God. Saint Augustine and Jean-Jacques Rousseau are the great masters of confession, but the difference was that the Bishop of Hippo recounted his life before God, and the writer only before himself!

As soon as we place ourself before God, opening ourself to Him without even looking for an answer, the transformation of our being begins. As long as we speak to ourselves, we become like a serpent trying to eat its own tail. To tell what is going on in us, objectively, without passion, to snatch our feelings and thoughts from the vicious circle of the self — this is one of the steps of prayer. This is well known to psychoanalysis, which took the principle of this form of prayer from the teaching of the Church. It is better for the soul to blame God, even, than to hold back what it feels. *"Out of the depths have I cried unto Thee, O Lord."* [1]

This conversation is good only when it is absolutely sincere: when it is neither excuses, nor eloquent humility. God is the 'Friend of man.' [2] He knew us before we were born. And progressively, through our own monologue, we shall be mysteriously helped, even though it still seems to us like a mental monologue ... as if the interior voice had not been heard. If we have conscientiously laid our trouble before the invisible God, the reply will emerge from what we say, and even if the interior voice does not emerge, the state of our soul will be clarified, calmed and harmonized.

John Chrysostom and Maximus the Confessor relate this prayer-conversation to the nervous system: they say it should take the place of our irritability so as to regulate our feeling.

The love of God, first fruit of prayer

For Saint Isaac the Syrian, [3] the first fruit of prayer is love for God. One who prays ardently raises his spirit, attains contemplation, and in contemplation the desire to love God is born. Love for God is acquired in prayer, and it is prayer which provides the motive for loving God. [4] For it is almost impossible to love God. Let us be frank! Without grace we would see no reason to love God, (I am speaking of people in general.) Our lot is hard, often unpleasant, and if it is pleasant we are not satisfied, for it is our nature to be dissatisfied. So should we not rather be annoyed with God?

Atheism is often rooted in man's revolt against injustice. Our innate sense of justice cannot resolve the problem of justice in itself — for what is justice? We are thrust into the agonizing dilemma between the divine goodness and the apparent injustice of the world, and, unable to hold out in the battle between these two poles, we prefer to decide that justice is absent, instead of saying: 'Perhaps I do not understand the goodness of God, nor true justice.'

Christ knew so well that mankind would be faced with this problem that he tells us: *"Let your light so shine before men, that they may see your good works, and glorify your Father which is in heaven"*[5] that is, they will recognize the fatherhood of God. Most people need the goodness of disciples in order to discern the ineffable goodness of the Master. If the image is good, they think, the Original will be all the more so. The compassion shown by a Christian makes people accept the mercy of the God of the Christians. But let us not deceive ourselves, God can only be grasped through inner experience.

Saint Isaac the Syrian explains to us that prayer is the only means of giving our heart the motivation for loving God. I will repeat that I am not speaking of beings in whom this arises spontaneously. I am speaking to those who do not possess this gift and for whom some method of prayer is necessary. But at the same time, those who love without effort are subject to change.

How then will prayer give rise to the desire to love? Because prayer is the source of knowledge of the '*many and immaterial*' planes, as Saint Isaac called them, and because the knowledge which gives the answer to our problems depends on prayer. The greatest vision of the divine Glory, the Transfiguration, came in the night during a long prayer.

Wait patiently

But let us follow the path indicated by Isaac the Syrian: *"To abide with patience in prayer means that man must renounce himself,"* and further on he adds: *"unceasing prayer will keep the mind from all impurity."*

"Abide," this is the keyword. Certainly there are prayers in which the soul is carried away by an impulse, where it calls out. There are others which last one, two, three hours. To 'abide' means to establish oneself in prayer as in one's house, to enter its atmosphere and then remain there.

"With patience": why? Prayer, the food of our soul, is disturbed at first by so many troubles. It seems not to be feeding us, or if it is, it suddenly becomes ineffective and bores us. Remember how Teresa of Avila spread her fingers slightly in order to look at the clock and see if the prayer time was nearly over. Prayer makes us discover in an uncomfortable way all the goings and comings in our inner waiting room. The essential thing, then, is to "abide with patience," and slowly the fruit will ripen from which prayer will flow like fresh and tranquil water. This fruit is the renunciation of self. Moralists are too anxious to track down the pride, vanity, egoism or humility in the soul... This

is true, but these various feelings are so mixed together in the human being that attentive examination of his conscience more often involves the risk of misleading him or making him fall by the wayside.

When we abide patiently in prayer, we become aware that it is impossible to pin down our feelings, and that this capricious and temperamental lass which is our 'me' — our capricious 'me,' to be more precise — is gradually losing its authority. Behind her tyranny, we see her for what she really is.

Prayer places man in a brutal consciousness of objective things.

The prayer of the name of Jesus, and transcending the 'me'

Let us take the simplest prayer, the Jesus Prayer: *"Lord Jesus Christ, Son of God, have mercy on me."* Set it alongside our 'me': they have nothing to do with one another.

"Have mercy on me!": the mental self will exclaim at once: *"But this is egoism — why not say have mercy on us! Why wish for my salvation, my forgiveness, without including others?"* Or else he will think: *"Yes, I am a sinner, but I do not need compassion."* The sinner feels the wounding of his pride by sin more keenly than the desire for divine mercy. Priests find this attitude in those who come for confession. Penitents are more impressed by those faults which hurt their dignity, and they hardly notice the real sins. Spiritual fathers sometimes ask people to write down their sins, and the penitent is almost always profoundly surprised to see that sin which he hardly considered is pointed out as grave. It is this which makes Saint Paul say: *"I judge nobody, but you, do not judge yourselves, for you cannot."*[6]

Patient prayer forces us to objectify ourselves. These words: *"Lord Jesus Christ, have mercy on me,"* will at first be alien to us. One of the words may touch us, but that will not express the prayer as a whole. Certain souls will want to repeat: *"Have mercy."* Others will feel a certain exaltation in repeating the name of Jesus, but the prayer in itself should transcend these states of the soul.

It is in repeating it, continuing it patiently, that we will overcome our limiting self, first identifying ourselves with the words. Then, we will come out of our limited selves, and our inner intelligence (*nous*) will be poured out from its mixture in many things.

Liturgical prayer transformed

It is the same with liturgical prayer. It teaches the faithful to master their capricious and temperamental moods. A person is sad, choked with financial worries, sick: he goes to the Easter service and has to sing of the Resurrection. He is happy to be alive; his heart is full of joy: or it is Good Friday, and he has

4

to sing lamentations before God who was crucified by men. To enter into the liturgical rhythm is to accustom oneself not to always live in one's own little myth, changing one's direction with every impression, but to live as the One true Man — the Second Adam — rejoicing and weeping with humanity.

Let us attach ourselves patiently to the rhythm of the prayer. The liturgical forms shape and transform.

Our society has known very well how to make use of this principle in constructing its secular liturgy. What a happy liturgy is that of the 'Big Stores,' and how great is their influence! It is this which has created the 'season of white goods' and useful gifts ... The 'iconographers' of the shop windows work over their displays with labour and imagination.

On the other hand, in our churches the liturgical periods have been weakened. We often find that the Christmas crib has lost its freshness; an Easter candle is modestly hidden behind the altar, and the Christian Feasts — the living memory of the events in the life of the Saviour — serve us simply as vacations.

Prayer as a source of knowledge

Saint Isaac continues his analysis of prayer: *"Prayer is the root of multiple and immaterial knowledge ... God introduces this knowledge into the spirit of one who prays."*

All knowledge is impaired by the waves of passion which erupt from inside and outside us, crossing and blocking our view. The character of these passionate elements is, on the one hand, to nourish our thought and action with something material, something dense, and, on the other hand, with something falsely unique, an idea or feeling which is imposed on us from outside. On the contrary, the intelligence formed in prayer becomes immaterial, one in its immateriality, while at the same time opening up many possibilities which free our intelligence, whereas the passions enslave it. Prayer is the root of this immaterial knowledge, because it accustoms us not to think, or more precisely, not to be thought.

What should we do with feelings and thoughts which assail us in spite of ourselves? Let them pass like a motion picture; consider them as objects in a shop window and take no account of what we feel toward them, but: *"Abide in prayer with patience."*

The new knowledge which will be born of this prayer will no longer be related to our thoughts and feelings. It will be given by God directly and will resemble what one might call 'knowledge-ignorance', without curiosity, and without possession of the objects which it knows, in the image of this patient prayer which moves towards the ineffable Trinity.

PRACTICAL EXERCISES TO CHAPTER ONE

The divine 'I':

The central idea of the first chapter is the divine 'I' which is won by prayer-conversation. The aim of this chapter is to rediscover the centre of the world: which is GOD.

Nowadays, especially in the West, everything is centred on man. Modern civilization is anthropocentric, while the a.b.c. of the spiritual life is theocentrism. That is why the practical exercises of the first chapter, given the level of human consciousness in our time, will demand greater efforts than in times past, when civilisation was theist and not humanist. Yet the reader should not be discouraged!

1) a) Make a faithful self-analysis, noting in writing the problems or desires which are real, immediate, and which command your attention (health, metaphysics, family, God, career, etc), and formulate them in the most precise way.

b) Do your best to put them in hierarchical order, underlining the most urgent or persistent. (Do not hesitate to recognize, if it is so, that 'beefsteak' preoccupies you more than God.)

2) Discern what power you rely upon to spontaneously resolve or satisfy your desires: intelligence, will, intuition, prayer, or an outside source of help such as the Church, a master, a spiritual father, the Gospel, science...

3) a) Having thus cleared the ground, put your problems and desires before God as fully and consciously as possible, placing yourself before Him, putting yourself at His disposal, submitting yourself to His will and asking Him to use — despite their relativity — the powers upon which you have relied.

b) Turned towards Him in this way, repeat this action at least seven times without looking for immediate results. After the seventh time, note the results, and then take up the exercise again every day or once week, once a month, or even once a year. (The more frequently it is done, the more effective it will be.) Let every act, every thought, every feeling gravitate around the universal centre: God.

4) Do not forget that the essential thing is to place the problems before God, not to solve them.

Questions To Ask Yourself

1) What are my urgent problems and desires?
2) On what power do I ultimately rely?
3) Have I opened myself to God seven times?
4) What results have I obtained?

NOTES

[1] Psalm 130:1.

[2] "Friend of man", *philanthropos*: a name for God commonly used by the Fathers of the Church.

[3] Saint Isaac the Syrian (probably 4th-5th centuries), spiritual writer and ascetic, considered second only to Saint John Climacus (7th Century Abbot of Sinai, author of the *"Ladder of Divine Ascent."*), in the Orthodox world, particularly in the monasteries. The current trend is to identify him with a Nestorian bishop of Nineveh who later became a hermit. The Orthodox world has for a long time resisted this confusion, but no proven evidence exists for one side or the other. Cf. Isaac the Syrian, *The Ascetical Homilies*, Holy Transfiguration Monastery, Boston, 1984.

[4] Saint Isaac the Syrian.

[5] Matthew 5:16

[6] 1 Corinthians 4:4-5. Translations vary, but several English translations include a phrase close to: *'but He that judges me is the Lord.'*

CHAPTER TWO

INNER PEACE

"Let us be silent"

"In peace let us pray to the Lord." With these words the Church begins its litanies.[8]

Before we start any prayer, monastic books recommend placing oneself before God, and then establishing inner peace.

During the liturgy, we sing: "Let all human flesh be silent ... let us put aside all earthly thoughts."

"Let us be silent," the deacon commands at the solemn moments of the Liturgy.[9]

This peace, this silence are the necessary conditions for effective prayer. A person who begins to pray while he is agitated cannot pray. Certainly this peace and silence are not yet what the soul will achieve towards the end of its spiritual life, but I would call them a preparatory recollection, a positive 'step forward.' To write a letter we need a clean sheet of paper, not one that has been scribbled all over; it is difficult to paint on a canvas that has been painted on before. Prayer too calls for an interior cleanup.

The problem of recollection and peace therefore comes before prayer. Here is what usually happens: in the morning we try to pray; we are more dull than agitated; we are even drowsy, and our prayer drags. The Church knows this; it does not demand silence; on the contrary, it offers the opening psalms which wake the soul gradually, and then, advises us to use short prayers to divide the day. But if we cannot follow the liturgical rhythm of the Hours, how are we to pass from the hubbub of our thoughts to silence?

There are various methods which would be fruitful to experiment with, starting while we are still young.

The spectator

The most ancient method is that of the spectator. You are restless or distressed? Then stand back from the state of your soul and your external conditioning as if they belonged to someone else. Speak of yourself in the third person; give yourself a nickname, either a rather ridiculous one or a solemn name. In my own case, for instance, I will think: "*Today, Monseigneur*[10] *is more irritable than charitable.*" Saint Seraphim of Sarov[11] spoke of himself as *'poor Seraphim.'* This method should be practiced at good moments as well as bad. Indeed, if you have some success, if you have helped your brother, or even if you have raised someone from the dead, for everything depends on your capacities, then, more than ever, you should speak of yourself in the third person.

Marshall Foch declared that true soldiers were terribly afraid, and that one must accustom oneself not to be afraid of fear. Only the insensitive are without fear: they die heroically, thoughtlessly throwing themselves on the enemy, who will kill them before they have been able to act, so that they will have contributed nothing to the battle. Courage consists in having no fear of fear, of having the inward serenity not to be distressed by distress, of not having feelings about our own feelings. Let us watch ourselves as if we were spectators, we are not the centre of humanity ... let us just look at ourselves.

Make yourself empty

The second method is that of Ambrose of Optina:[12] "*Make nothing of yourself, so that God can make the universe of you.*" In other words, "*empty yourself*"; stop thoughts, desires and judgements about others — and about yourself.

Are you capable of sitting and suddenly doing nothing, being nothing? Well, that is perfect. But I have the impression that it is not easy, for immediately images and concerns rush in. Then think: "*All that I have done, all that I am doing, all that I should do, all that I have not done, is of no importance, and if I should stay in my present state for eternity, God be praised!*"

Empty your inner being; arrive at nothingness.

The two possibilities

Very close to this is the third method, that of the *two possibilities*. One of the disquieting things in human life is choice. Man can choose the spiritual or the material life; in sickness he can get well or die, and so on. These two possibilities stir up trouble, and the greatest trouble they create is hesitation. The Fathers teach us never to stop in indecision between two paths. He who hesitates is a perpetual deserter. In war there are two means of not being killed: to attack, or to run, and certainly anyone who asks himself whether to attack or retreat will be killed. Confronted with your sin, the most dangerous attitude is hesitation.

Choice faces us with two alternative decisions. The first: I choose what is easy for me; I give up the perfect, spiritual and monastic life; I occupy myself with business; God will forgive me; I choose a small bourgeois way. The second: I choose prayer and Christ, doing away with comfort, vehicles and quietude.

This choice seems easy at first sight. Believe me, it is not. Most of the time a human being is made up of such a variety of feelings, 'complexes,' as our modern language would say, that he has not the power to totally choose his aim. Saint John of Kronstadt [13] said that one should throw oneself into this decision as into the fire, and Monseigneur Winnaert[14] declared in one of his sermons that in order to move towards holiness it was enough to say: From this moment on I am throwing myself into holiness — but we do not do this. If we do choose, then such is human nature that a throng of contrary arguments rush in at once.

In sin or holiness, the way of decision is that of great beings. It is only valid if we patiently sacrifice everything for the goal.

Renunciation of choice

There is another way to attain peace before prayer: to accept both possibilities, to entrust oneself to God. This is not hesitation, but a 'renunciation of choice.' Tomorrow I shall be rich? I accept it. I shall be poor? I accept it. I am a failure or a genius? As God wills. Repeating this phrase will give us peace.

So that is the third method, after those of the spectator and emptiness — to renounce a choice when it offers itself. You can even help your soul within by thinking that lack of success is as useful in God as a success that is against His will, and that you can strengthen yourself by the example of certain lives that were called failures, but which were spiritually superior to so many others judged as marvellous. How many people are dead while they live in abundance or success?

So it is necessary to nod to both possibilities: I shall welcome this day, be it lucky or unlucky. I used the words lucky and unlucky. I have noticed that the influence of astrology or other sciences of the lucky and unlucky diminishes many souls by plunging them into unrest. I recognize that this tension has sometimes been able to develop the sensitivity of certain spirits, and that Providence often makes the best of ambiguity, but it is also certain that this brings the danger of impaired judgement.

I know that we are so accustomed to stretching our soul towards something that it is difficult for us to accept the emptiness, or to stop in what is neither past nor present, in the 'I am nothing.' In this connection, perform an experiment. Think: *"if I am commanded to make circles on the Place de la Concorde or to plant a tree with its roots in the air, I will do it."* Ah! If you can internally do anything, no matter what, if you can strip yourself of the useless 'common sense' which destroys our intelligence, then you are nothing. Do not be mistaken; intelligent people do not 'think.' From the moment one starts to 'think' — in the ordinary sense of the word — one is not intelligent. Are those who love deeply distracted by small desires? A Russian proverb teaches us that only geese and cretins think.

Unfortunately, we cannot ask everybody not to think. Without doubt you have noticed that stupid people think a great deal. They stew; they judge; they compound; they react; they protest; they approve; their mind is always in motion.

Fasten on a fixed idea

The Church offers us a fourth method: *to fasten on a fixed idea*. It is a form of stubbornness, the principle of the repeated prayer, of the rosary, but with a thought. Let us assume that what matters to me is to pronounce the name of Jesus six hundred times a day, or to apply myself for so many minutes to such and such a thought. Once I have set this single goal, everything else will lose its importance. This leads us to balance and, so simply, rids us of restlessness.

Nothing is owed to me

Let us finally add the fifth and last method: this is to engrave on our spirit the attitude that *nothing is owed to me*.

Agitations in general have their source in the claim that something or other is owed to us, or that humanity ought to deal with us in some special manner. Claims like these are the soil of unrest. *"What! He has abandoned me. He has not recognized the good that I have done for him! I am being treated unjustly. God does not understand me!"* And the crisis arises. But if you consider that nothing is owed to you, neither salvation, nor health, nor friendship; if you marvel at the fact that you have eyes to see, a mouth to kiss or eat with, and that, more than this, you are standing upright; if you can make a list of the gifts received, and respond: *"Goodness, I am still here"*; then a serenity that knows no twilight will rise within your heart.

11

A single expression of Christ brings these five methods together: *"Blessed are the poor in spirit."*[15]

In reality, anyone who looks at himself as a spectator strips himself; anyone who empties himself strips himself; anyone who decides or who entrusts himself to God strips himself; anyone who takes only the essential strips himself; to say nothing of the last one, he who claims nothing. This is poverty in spirit.

Never forget that the law of progress in spiritual life is neither to submit one's soul to theoretical judgements, nor to one's own use. I shall explain what I mean. From the objective point of view it is accurate to conceive, for example, that when one has worked all one's life for one's family, it would be normal if they recognized that. Yes, this view is accurate, but your soul will be troubled by it. It is when you get beyond this kind of objective judgement that you will become capable of prayer.

Let us gradually arrive at the point where we are not touched by the world of values of the passions, of metaphysics, and of philosophy. Let us penetrate to the heart of the interior world of balance and peace. This last requires, at least provisionally, that we sacrifice the judgement which is called objective. Consider the paradox of a saint who, having attained the summit of humanity, regards himself — and this very sincerely — as an 'abortion'.[16] Speaking with a sinner foul with sin, he judges himself inferior to him. It is undeniable that this spiritual plane necessitates non-judgement. One who sets up the following list: *"I am young; he is not. I am chaste; he is dissolute. I have given my fortune to the poor; he exploits the unhappy."* will automatically arrive at the following conclusion: *"He is a sinner, and I am much less of one than he is."* This will be the truth, but it will put an immediate stop to his spiritual life. A fertile antinomy is to consider that spiritual growth has nothing to do with judgement! Must we then reject judgement? No, it will reappear in the strengthened soul on an authentically objective plane which will no longer trouble the soul. Let us not ask the metaphysical why; let us adopt the attitude which gives serenity and peace so that suddenly prayer may swell its buds and open out.

What matters the conquest of the whole world if our soul is damaged? In this, our soul ranks higher than the universe.

Attention! Here comes the trickster. He will cunningly ask you: *"So the salvation of your soul is higher?"* Answer, *"No, the salvation of my soul is not superior to the world, but working on my soul may well be."* The conception of the salvation of the soul has been distorted. People imagine that the performance of certain actions leads to 'Paradise.' No, what leads to Paradise is the desire to sacrifice certain things in order to rest in inner peace, and that cannot be egoism, for I know that my soul does not belong to me, that it has been entrusted to me and I am only a craftsman.

Perseverance

I shall finish these few sketches of the different methods of finding peace by underlining the fact that everything succeeds because of perseverance. Man knows this consciously and unconsciously, and a great number of novels and films illustrate it. The modern parable of the seeker for petrol whose obstinacy is rewarded is one of the images. Even when hope is receding, we must continue or begin again. The Gospel is exact: *"The deserter leaves at the crucial moment; one who perseveres to the very end will be saved."*[17]

In fact, these methods do not give immediate results; the results are not rapid. But let us examine what obstructs us, just as a conscientious engineer would do. Each person personally constructs his soul; others can only offer advice or give a push here and there. And although the teaching of the saints is a universal teaching, each gives it in his own way. There is no general rule. This is why our Lord warns us: *"I shall come like a thief; none will know the hour and the day."*[18]

Everything is gratis, since God comes when He wishes, but everything is in some way earned and conquered, because it is to him who takes that God gives. A last piece of advice: Do not let go of prayer, even if it bores you. Choose or receive a simple formula for your convenience and hold firm to it! Spiritual life does not erupt through your impressions and emotions. Oh no! It advances in us silently, like a natural, biological element that we become aware of only when it is taken away.

These different methods are happily summed up in a phrase from Origen: *"Before praying, relax and rediscover silence."* These are only proposals, only instruments. Every one of them is more or less suited to a different temperament.

In the technique of prayer, two dangers are hidden which must be foreseen: results that seem to be too swift, or too slow. Certain categories of souls begin unceasing prayer, practice it, persevere, and nothing comes; they grow tired and they turn away. On the other hand, there are others who obtain immediate results and are invaded by unexpected phenomena, by warmth of heart, or exaltation. In actual fact, those who have great difficulty are no less privileged than their opposites. The two possibilities have a dual aspect. If slowness leads to discouragement, easy success can create imbalance, because it brings results before the soul has been prepared by inward transformation. The spiritual wine needs to be baptized with a little water.

Simplicity of heart

All this shows us that the peace that prepares us for prayer is not absolute peace, but that we should seek a preliminary tranquility. These methods are therapeutic; they are to help the soul overcome instability. They complete and confirm one another. Let us go back to the method of the 'spectator,' for example. It harbours the danger of theatricality, because to look at one's sufferings is novel and agreeable. In self-observation, we are the stage director and the actor of our soul, and this cannot be avoided. There is just one remedy for this: to strain towards simplicity of heart. Saint Gregory the Theologian says with harshness but with justice: *"To see oneself as a great sinner is pleasant, and it is equally enjoyable to see oneself as a saint or a genius, but to see oneself as one is, neither too high nor too low, seems mediocre."* Yet it is in this that the strength of the method of the spectator lies.

Absence of judgement

Another remark: the soul standing in prayer registers impressions quite quickly; this sensitivity is found in relation to both the external and internal worlds. The Fathers therefore advise us to have a dispassionate attitude, one that registers images without reacting to them. Today you are in hell, tomorrow in front of Christ; today is lucky; tomorrow is unlucky; it does not matter; so listen, yet do not draw conclusions. This is a tremendous apprenticeship, not to judge one's own situation! I would even say, not to set a value on it but simply to see it. You can address yourself to a spiritual father, but be ready to defer to him when he shows you as tragic something which appears trivial to you, and if he does not take a grave view of what seems to you tragic. Here, we should give up judging for ourselves.

Entry into the interior life is accompanied by a throng of impressions, signs and propitious or baleful voices which can precipitate the soul into madness. Beware! The person who leaves behind sensual, bourgeois and habitual conceptions encounters unknown landscapes. He or she will be without any point of reference or common ground, in a world that has no firm criteria. One of the dangerous forms is the swing between what I have already called lucky and unlucky, between God and the devil, sadness and joy, true and untrue, and still more dangerous is all judgement of oneself that thinks: "I am good, or I am bad." Beware! Register; only register. Outside the health and tradition of the Church, entry into the interior life can unbalance a person.

Disclosing our thoughts

This is why one principle of all the 'startzi,' from Saint John the Evangelist to this day, proves so excellent: the disclosing of thoughts.

This principle is not far from psychoanalysis. The psychoanalysts didn't invent anything: it is a matter of telling, of telling oneself or of telling God what is going on in one, without comment, simply speaking objectively: *"I would like ... to kill, to die, to pray. Is it good, is it bad? Am I to blame or am I innocent? True or false? I do not concern myself with that."*

I will repeat that, in the spiritual life, what appears true may be false, and that is natural. We live with external data which are neither true nor false, but which have become habitual, become customary for us: to obey mamma; to shake hands with those we meet; to go to church; to earn a living. That is how it is. The whole of mankind lives in obedience to conditions and laws which it has accepted, conditions and laws which are entirely relative, often questionable, and certainly not absolute! But they contribute to an external equilibrium. Conceived as a result of experience, even though they are imperfect, they are seals of stability. We have an image of them in reforms of children's education. The Americans, declaring that we must not oppose children in anything, let their children go beyond bounds, and sometimes they come to crime. Of course, the use of the whip and the too harsh disciplines of earlier times were also at fault. It is not easy to strike the right balance.

Accepting without judging

We are apprentices in the spiritual life, and less than apprentices as we surrender to a new experience, to the rhythm of prayer. Let us, like reporters — reporters who want to be serious; reporters on the threshold of an unknown society — give ear and be extremely prudent. The process of comprehending a people is identical to that of comprehending the inner world; each requires great patience. First we observe customs, without the least prejudice, just as we would observe the life of butterflies, and then it is only after we have given up weighing its values that we can sketch the first judgement. You have to transform your old supermarket, or 'Uniprice', into a temple of prayer. The difference between the 'Uniprice' and the Church is that the former estimates the value of all merchandise before buying, while the latter accepts without judging.

When our Lord declares: *"Do not judge and you will not be judged."*[19] He is speaking primarily of the judgement we make of our brother, but we also are our own brother. This is why a true confession is so rare. In twenty years of ministry I have only heard two or three true confessions; the others came out of the Uniprice. Most penitents arrive at confession with their personal solution; the priest is only expected to agree.

PRACTICAL EXERCISES

The personal 'I':

The basic idea of the first chapter was theocentrism; that of the second is the method of rediscovering the personal 'I' by freeing it from our aggressive selves and from external conditioning.

1) Experiment with the five techniques of interior peace:
> the spectator
> making an emptiness
> the two possibilities, or the renunciation of choice
> concentration on one idea
> "nothing is owed to me"

Apply each of these five techniques for about five minutes (25 minutes in all) to restlessness, worries, trials.

2) Repeat this experiment at least seven times, and note the results.

3) Note the technique which seems the most effective, without rejecting the others.

4) Persevere in this technique until the day when the 'I' becomes transcendent to all influences.

Questions to ask yourself

1) Have I tried the experiment?
2) What kind of restlessness, worry, or trials have I applied it to?
3) Which of the five techniques is the most effective?

NOTES

[7] In the liturgy of Saint John Chrysostom.

[9] In the liturgy of Saint Germain of Paris.

[10] The original text, written two years before the consecration of the future Mgr. Jean, had "Monsieur the Archpriest."

[11] 1759-1833 — one of the most venerated and loved of recent Orthodox saints.

[12] Ambrose of Optina (1812-1891), the *staretz* or spiritual father, was, with Saint Seraphim of Sarov, undoubtedly the most popular of 19th Century Russia. Optina, or Optina Pustin was, throughout the century, under the direction of successive *startzi* — Leonid (1768-1841), Macarius (1788-1860) and Ambrose — the high-point of the renaissance of traditional Orthodox spirituality in Russia after the destructive reforms of Peter the Great. A renewal of monasticism in eremetic form but open to pilgrims in search of spiritual counsel, and it was the diffusion of hesychast spirituality, based on the practice of the "prayer of the name of Jesus." Through many different publications (more than 125 works in the one century), Ambrose took a major role in this double work. It was he who translated Saint John Climacus' *Ladder of Spiritual Ascent* into Russian, and he also received 2-300 people every year.

[13] Saint John of Kronstadt, recognised as a saint during his lifetime, was permanently surrounded by an innumerable crowd of pilgrims and penitents, drawn by the renown of the cures and conversions he obtained. Read his spiritual journal, *"My Life in Christ."*

[14] 1880-1937, precursor of the Orthodox Catholic Church of France. His meeting with Eugraph Kovalevsky in 1936 was the determining factor for the renaissance of Western Orthodoxy in France.

[15] Matthew 5: 3.

[16] A reference to Saint Paul, who described himself in a similar way: I Corinthians 15.

[17] Mark 13:13 ; see also Luke 21: 19.

[18] A reference to Luke 12: 39-40. Matthew 24:43-51. Also see Thessalonians 5:2.

[19] Matthew 7:1.

CHAPTER THREE

PRAYER AS FOOD

Food for the body, for the soul, for the spirit

The body needs to eat and breathe in order not to die; health is based on air and good food. On the other hand, we can live without seeing — a blind man lives; without hearing — a deaf person lives; without perceiving perfumes and flavours — we still live just the same. It is the same with the spiritual life; it is sustained by food-prayer and breath-prayer. As for visions, hearing voices, sensations, they count for little. Often souls that are dazzled by apparitions and psychic phenomena are so captivated that they forget the wholesome food and forget to breathe the good spiritual air. Perhaps they are visionaries, but they are sick and half-mad.

Food-prayer and breath-prayer reveal the essentials of human anthropology to us. Man is composed of three elements: spirit (pneuma), soul (psyche) and body (soma).

What is the food of the body? Whether it is vegetables, meat, or fish, it is communion with the cosmos, with animals and plants, contact with nature which penetrates us, communion with the universe. The need to eat in order to live is also the mystery of the unity of nature, if I may say so, it is a 'natural Mass'.

The food of the soul is composed of relationships with beings, cultures, arts. As far as food is concerned, our epoch particularly prizes a healthy diet. Everywhere people are speaking of naturism, vegetarianism and so on! But no one is interested in a diet for the soul. Yet books are a kind of food: devoured without discernment they cause a disorder, anxiety, which could be described as due to 'lack of hygiene.' We certainly do not observe fasts of the soul! Rather we contrive to provide ourselves with indiscriminate overindulgence: an omnivorous Reader's Digest. If its taste is well developed, our palate does not eat just anything; but consider your soul: it swallows anything, music, films, books, meetings. Hygiene of the psyche is absent. I will give you an example from one of the saints. The Virgin appeared to him and he perceived that she remained at the door of his cell. He asked her: "Queen of heaven, why do you not come in? I know that I am unworthy." And the Virgin replied: "Too many of the books in your library are useless. When you have burned them, I will come in."

God is the sole food of our spirit, and He communicates Himself to us only through prayer. Neither human contact, nor books, nor thoughts, nor feelings, nor what belongs to culture, to civilization, or to religion, will feed that which is divine in us. Only the Divine, God, can feed the divine.

People sometimes wonder why Christ, the God-man, spent nights in prayer. It was because He was spirit, soul and body. He nourished his body with food; He nourished his soul with contemplation of flowers, with conversation with the Apostles, with friendship ... He nourished His spirit with prayer. He prayed not because he needed to ask anything of His Father, He who knew everything, but to nourish His spirit.

Without prayer, the spirit wilts and dies: the body lives; the soul is moved; but the spirit is dead. Prayer is the indispensable, the vital food. Nevertheless, to advance in prayer we must learn to choose the form of our prayer, or at least we must be simple enough to come to it naturally: perpetual, interior, liturgical, with or without words, etc. We shall try to look at all this in the course of this book.

The different methods which we have presented all help us to reach the state of readiness to pray. This is not yet prayer; it is a state, while prayer itself is an interior action.

Sincere prayer

Now a great misunderstanding looms.

Some people say: I prefer prayer that comes from the heart to mechanical prayers, or to prayers which contradict my nature and my feelings; so why should I pray when I feel like dancing?

The problem is this: That it is only rarely that a person finds himself in a state of sincere prayer: this is a direct or indirect gift of God, who suddenly grants him the possibility to pray, or external circumstances which lift him — the fervent desire for something; this sincere prayer will not be the true nature, the constant food of this person; he will not be a praying being, but a being who prays.

Saint Seraphim of Sarov cites a classic example taken from an old text: a child's coffin is being transported (in those days the lid of the coffin was not screwed down until it reached the cemetery); behind the coffin walked a weeping widow. A prostitute is passing by in the same street, and, seeing this spectacle, she stops the procession and cries: *"Lord, if I am punished for my wicked actions, I understand it, but that You take the child of this honest widow ... I pray Thee, restore him to life."* And the child comes back to life.

Let us analyze this prayer: it is absolute and sincere, first because this woman possesses faith and humility; prostitutes often have more faith than others, as their behaviour plunges them into humility so that they consider themselves unworthy. This woman could have been indignant at God: "You have no right..." but her total humility suppresses every demand in her. Moreover, the stifled maternity of this prostitute bursts out in a simple way, with such psychic power that she is heard. This is a prayer-gift, filled with maternal love. A series of motives have helped this woman to bring forth a prayer which brought about the revival of the child although she was not a saint.

We may say 'sincere' or 'insincere', but this woman of the street did not ask herself whether her prayer was sincere or not. Everything joined as if at a geometric point: maternity, humility, faith, ardour. Her prayer is sincere because all the elements of her soul are conformed to it, when as soon as we pray we find many hindrances in ourselves.

In general, the word 'sincere' is extremely ambiguous. How many people say: "I am sincere." What does it mean? They imagine themselves to be sincere. "I do not hide my opinion, I say just what I think, I am sincere"; if we start to scratch the surface, the superficiality of this state is revealed; it is only a casual passing feeling. What 'self' is speaking just then? — the dignity of Mr. Dupont, his wounded pride, an impulse of his psyche. It is sincere towards this 'I',[20] towards one of his 'I's. This sincerity is not sincerity, but merely hypocrisy, an inferior element dominating our being.

The essential obstacle is our instability. In social life we shut out intruders; we cut our bridges with those who annoy us, but we do not know how to drive away painful impressions or how to stop thoughts. We are weak. And we have not even become aware that we should drive them away. The Theosophists teach that good thoughts create good feelings and vice versa, but I tell you that the Church teaches that we should get rid of both good and bad elements, not keep them in mind.

Long prayer or short prayer?

The question first posed in Holy Scripture seems contradictory: "Do not pray like the hypocrites and the Pharisees, showing off with grand speeches,"[21] yet suddenly the words of the Apostle Paul: "Pray without ceasing,"[22] seem to invite us to the long services and the unceasing prayer of hesychasm. If we want to say it conscientiously, the Lord's Prayer is long and difficult; yet it is Christ who gave it to us.

Long or short prayer? Our Lord declares that we must not imitate the Pharisees who pray long, yet He Himself spends the night in prayer. His conduct is that of those who pray unceasingly.

Let us first see what is petitionary prayer. It is certain that the best formula for petitionary prayer is brief: "God, revive him, Amen," or "God save me, Amen"; or even a rising of the soul in silence. The requests of the litanies are short; they remind us, yet they do not 'install' themselves in us. So, will you answer me, why pray long?

Because it is difficult to make the short, unique, efficacious prayer burst out from our soul, we prolong our prayers ... this is not to make them longer, but simply to catch the short prayer. All prayers should lead to the prayer of silence. It is perfect when the heart prays without words.

Saint John of Kronstadt, after torrents of praises to God, succeeded in curing sickness with a phrase or a gesture. Effective short prayer is reached through long prayer.

Saint Macarius the Great [23] says that prayer is an invitation. We clean the interior, set the table, and the guest comes. But if he is already present, we do not repeat: 'Come again.' We no longer invite the guest who is already with us. Prayer is not measured by length, but by quality. Two hours of prayer are not necessarily better than one second.

Undoubtedly we could say that Christ condemns the prayer of the Pharisee; this is because the latter is really listening to himself and admiring himself, whereas the Publican waits for divine mercy.[24] Grandiloquence is the gravest danger in the spiritual life. If the soul begins to give ear, whether to his virtues or his vices, he is automatically talking with himself: good, bad, joyous or tragic, it will be a prayer which listens to itself. As he blessed God, the Pharisee was looking at himself; as he beseeched God: "Lord, have mercy," the Publican effaced himself, lost in the corner of the temple.

The meaning of perpetual prayer is the same as that of long prayers. On the one hand it checks wandering thought as the spirit concentrates; on the other hand, it guides us towards the moment when the lips no longer pronounce words, when the prayer flows without interruption. All this can happen only after the castle of prayer is built, which is a serenity and tranquility whose doors are closed to spiritual 'tramps,' whether these are dressed in magnificent ideas and sublime visions or in carnal thoughts and petty restlessness.

Food-prayer and breath-prayer

We come now to food-prayer and breath-prayer.

As I have already said, prayer is the food and breath of the spirit. It is not only praise of God; it is the nourishment of our spirit, which falls asleep and loses life without it.

Food-prayer and breath-prayer are fundamentally different.

Man does not eat without ceasing; he eats two or three times a day. He eats, then he digests, and finally he assimilates. Food-prayer is like this; useful prayer to take at regular intervals, once, twice, or three times a day, after which it should be digested and assimilated if it is to give results.

On the contrary, we breathe as long as we live, and our breathing does not stop, day or night. Normal breath is regular and rhythmic. But air that is too strong can lead to sickness of the lungs, and may be entirely unsuitable to a highly spiritual life.

To be really nourishing, food-prayer should not only be petition or praise, but also meditation and confession: a thought, a passage of Scripture, a phrase of adoration: let us take hold of this with our mind. Thus, in "Lord, Thou art great," let the word 'great' remain in us. It need not necessarily be addressed to 'Thee'; the spirit can think "God is great" just as well as "Thou art great." And when it enters us, it is not at all necessary to understand it at once by breaking it up and analyzing it; let us simply let it rest until it is assimilated into our spirit. Often the answers will come much later!

This prayer should be adapted to our being; it may last a quarter of an hour a day, or as long as six hours uninterrupted. Certain monks take it up every three hours; others practice it several times an hour.

Prayer and meditation

This prayer gives rise to meditation. But please note! The term 'meditation' is ambiguous, just like 'sincere'. Frequently used in the literature, it needs to be qualified or clarified. People think that to meditate is to embroider around a chosen theme. The imagination is set into action and creates the desired climate without delay. You meditate on the light, and everything becomes luminous; you walk on your toes; your wings open. But the least accident of your life will lamentably destroy this world of paradisiac appearance. Or you are an intellectual turned towards the rational; then you compose an ingenious hierarchy: the divine light, the angelic light, the profane light, the sacred light; you write it down in a good book, a very good book ... but this too will be artificial. Such meditations have succeeded, but when they fall into banality — for the soul is not always imaginative or intelligent — how many useless and questionable things take possession of it!

So, instead of 'meditate,' I prefer to say, 'grasp by the mental'. Do not hurry to go into this formula; it will explain itself and open out in you.

Food-prayer necessitates periods of prayer and assimilation. It contains a meditative element in the exact sense of the word: to listen attentively, to record, to be present, and that is it.

Discipline and balance

The great principle of this prayer is discipline: To feed oneself as regularly as possible, at the same hour, in the same circumstances, just as we do for our body: A healthy diet for the body, and a healthy diet for the spirit.

We must go beyond the error which confuses the psychic world of emotions with the spiritual. We admit that the machine depends on technology, that medicine is salutary for the body, and we think that the spirit escapes that. No! The spirit's nature is to organize, to vitalize, to transform, and the instrument of its formation is the nourishing prayer, giver of lost capacities, pouring forth the healthy life that precedes health: the spiritual health that precedes holiness.

I dare to believe that after you are accustomed to coming regularly to liturgical services, after a few months, a year, two years perhaps — that depends — you will suddenly discover something changed in you! A source of rhythm and balance! Our participation in the Church is the sole remedy capable of saving us from the heights and the depths, that is to say, from sickness. We go towards holiness by way of health; otherwise we could be saints today and criminals tomorrow. Evidently, artistic creation that touches sublime planes sometimes makes use of disorder, of illumination, but that is a different path, and what is its end?

PRACTICAL EXERCISES

Feeding the spirit:

Having centred your consciousness on God (Chapter One), and detached the 'self' from its conditioning (Chapter Two), it is now indispensable to feed the spirit.

1) Study this feeding:

a) Of the body: regulate fasts and abstinences and avoid excesses;

b) Of the soul: govern our relations with people, our choice of books, of music, etc...

c) Of the spirit: prayer

2) Introduce food-prayer (in liturgical form) at least twice a day, morning and evening; for example, say Lauds in the morning and Compline in the evening.

3) Apply yourself to pronouncing the words and grasping them mentally.

Questions to ask yourself

1) What is my food for the body, the soul, and the spirit?
2) What are my prayer-foods? What forms do they take?
3) What is the state of my consciousness during prayer?

NOTES

[20] The French has "moi".

[21] Matthew 6:5 and 7, and Luke 20:47.

[22] I Thessalonians 5:17.

[23] A father of the Church of the 4th Century, one of the organisers of monasticism in the Egyptian desert, where he was a hermit. Fifty spiritual homilies traditionally attributed to him form an important event in hesychastic spirituality as described in the *Philokalia* and in *Pseudo-Macarius, the fifty spiritual homilies and the Great letter*, Classics of Western Sprituality, Paulist Press, New York.

[24] The parable of the Pharisee and the Publican. Luke 18:9-14.

CHAPTER FOUR

BREATH-PRAYER

The original imbalance

The tragedy of original sin is that the world is turned upside down. The spirit should be nourished by God and breathe Him; the soul should be nourished by the spirit and breathe it; the body should be nourished by the soul and breathe it; and the world should be nourished by the human body and breathe it.

Having turned away from God, having turned its values upside down, cut off the contact between itself and the Creator — which is the first death — the human spirit lost its true nourishment and breathing. I said *nourishment* and *breathing*, and you have already guessed that this is because Christ said: *"I am your food,"* [25] and because the Holy Spirit is called Spirit, *Breath*, Air, Wind.

Having stopped this divine nourishment voluntarily, the human spirit has sought another nourishment, another form of breath, and has turned towards the levels of the psyche, giving birth to our civilizations as it did so. Our civilizations are an unhealthy phenomenon, just like our culture and our art, which are results of the human spirit feeding on things inferior to it. In reality, what does it desire, in friendship, in art, in music, in sociology? God! The demand of the spirit is absolute: culture, friendship and art do not correspond to its nature, hence the dissatisfaction and the drama of man's sorrows; hence his lack of balance. As his nourishment has been deprived of the divine salt, he goes from one illusion to another.

The psyche, the soul, is already weakened by the spiritual, which, itself deprived of the divine salt, the divine food, in some way of the 'blood'; the soul is deprived of its normal nourishment, that is, of the human spirit, which no longer nourishes but instead exploits it, so that the soul turns towards that which can provide it with a certain supplement. It takes refuge in matter. So we see that strange phenomenon of a complex world, the world of the psyche, caught up with the elements — which leave it hungry and arouse the passions. Diseases inevitably appear. The spirit saturated with psychism brings anxiety; how can a soul which eats its body not set loose diseases! What then can we say of the body which, instead of being the sun, the radiance, the nourishment of the cosmos, turns towards the cosmos and uses it more and more! Matter, finding nothing lower than itself to serve as nourishment, becomes anaemic; the doors of destruction and death open before it; the only nourishment offered is nothingness.

Restore prayer, and the equilibrium will be reestablished. But is it possible to reestablish the balance between the body and the soul when the soul is preyed upon by its superior, by the human spirit?

The healing of the spirit

First of all, we must heal the spirit by surrounding it with the proper hygiene. This vital hygiene is God, or, as it says in Genesis — 'the Tree of Life.'[26] This is why the two forms of prayer which feed the spirit are *food-prayer* and *breath-prayer*.

The reason for prayer, before the transformation of the world, is to bring man back to his original balance which was lost through sin.

Given that we do not know how to live in this reversal of values, that we are accustomed to seeing the superior drawing upon the inferior, the return is painful, and we find that the conquest of prayer is not easy. Nevertheless, it is with this that we can begin; this then brings into play a balance between spirit and soul, soul and body, and between the body and the cosmos. But in order to attain these balances, we must reorient our spirit towards the Source of Life.

Daily life regulates our nourishment by the clock: as far as possible we eat at fixed hours. We give our organism time for digestion. Our food is suited to our temperament and to our state of health; moreover, we want it to be natural, of good quality, etc... The same principle applies to prayer... to divine nourishment. A being whose interior song is as well regulated as his meals, according to the hours, gradually builds up spiritual health for himself.

On the contrary, breath-prayer should be continual — we breathe in sleep as well as in the waking state. It is therefore unceasing, perpetual, whether we are conscious or unconscious. Hesychasm is one of its results. Good breathing depends not only on sturdy lungs but also on the climate in which we live; a chemical factory or a dusty house makes us sick. Unceasing prayer is conditioned by the *spiritual climate*.

Liturgical prayer and interior prayer

The food-prayer par excellence is liturgical prayer; breath-prayer is interior prayer. We are equally incorrect whether we say that only breath-prayer or only food-prayer is necessary. Some people follow the whole liturgical rhythm: they eat spiritually; yet if they do not breathe God, they will be sick and asthmatic. Others, who breathe God, can go for a certain length of time without food, but they have no resistance against external life.

Christ had no need to call upon God, for He Himself was God; nevertheless he spent six hours in prayer in the evening. Critics in the 19th century wondered what He was doing! *He was feeding His spirit.* If He had not prayed, His human spirit would have been imperfect.

Some people imagine that for them music or the beauty of nature takes the place of prayer: this again confuses the spirit with the soul. They have the impression of being fed, but they are not fed by God. The divine point of the spirit plunges into God. Cosmic or artistic beauty give them the illusion of health, because in spite of everything the system of the psyche receives an element of beauty; but the spirit is beyond this, created by God for God alone.

These two forms of prayer are indispensable: liturgical prayer regulated by the Hours, and the unceasing interior liturgy carried by the breath-prayer. Breath-prayer does not necessarily mean that we have to fit it to physical inhalation and exhalation, any more than food-prayer must always be the Eucharist.

Balanced food-prayer

According to modern theory, physical nourishment is beneficial when it contains a variety of vitamins, calories, etc. Menus are calculated to follow diets. It is exactly the same with spiritual nourishment: culinary art, liturgical art.

One of the Church Councils of Africa declared that the liturgy rests on two principles: good taste, and truth. A liturgical form which impregnated the spirit with false ecstasy or which aroused feelings comparable to pride would not be authentic. This area conceals a great number of snares.

The traditions make use of many levels. They awaken the intellect by readings, the soul by poetic forms, images and music. If they only offered one food, the spirit would be impoverished; it is the total being which converges towards the spirit and so moves it towards God. The liturgical Hours provided by the religions are menus; they are preparations whose centre and only nourishment is God.

You wish to pray ... Let us suppose that you are alone; you pray for one hour, not mentally, but with your own words or those of already existing prayers; it is of no importance which. As in abstract art, it is not the subject which counts; it is the art itself. If you wish, spend some time on petition, praising God, penitence; blend the impulses, the thoughts; go deep into this or that divine mystery. The subject should exist, of course, but what should be absolute is that during this time you are facing God, for Him and in Him. Do not try to get a result. Practice an hour of prayer, as you choose, in order that your spirit and your soul should begin to eat, should be restored after a great famine, and then — excuse the phrase — afterward they can digest. They will recover strength even if they have become drowsy, as the apostles did when they were unable to endure Christ's long and powerful prayer.

Speaking of drowsiness, you often swallow sleeping medicines in order to relax your agitated life; pray, and you will see that at the second or third psalm you will fall asleep under the gaze of God.

Prayer, conscious or unconscious, nourishes our being. So much is it a presence that a pastor who lends his parish hall for the celebration of Orthodox services told me, not long ago, that in this hall 'one could take hold of it with one's hand.' It is true, in this ordinary room, prayer had built an invisible temple. In the image of this hall, our spirit adapts itself to prayer. We go through periods of 'digestion', when we are not thirsty for God. Instinct guides us in the material world because we live in the bosom of a distorted world, but in the bosom of the spiritual we have forgotten this instinct. As we lose our spiritual health, we no longer necessarily experience hunger for prayer. Nevertheless, if we become accustomed to the liturgies we will be hungry for them again.

We should not hope to achieve contemplation quickly. Some meals are served with champagne, others with ordinary wine, and others still with Vichy water; to have champagne every time would be tiring.

Food-prayer is linked with reading, with images, with singing if possible, and with meditation. It always depends on a number of aspects, for if you concentrated only on reading, for example, God would become a purely intellectual object; if only on an image, He would only be felt. The Living God would disappear.

Permanent breath-prayer

Breath-prayer should aim to become unceasing. Man is half-dead, half-alive. A condition for healing is fresh air. But beware of the danger! The Sermon on the Mount [27] says, in effect, that goodness rests in interiorization, in not submitting to external conditioning, but I have often noted a false kind of interiorization, in which the scrupulous individual creates a dismal and sad little world which revolves around his small 'self'. In that case the spiritual master will say on the contrary: *"Go out; busy yourself with other people. You have no access to God and the divine within you; you have access within you only to precisely what separates you from God and from others."*

Breath-prayer lives on pure air. Before entering it, brush away every narrow, every micro-psychic thought, as the Fathers call it. If your God is petty, your interior prayer is dangerous. Face your spirit with a spacious conception of God. The more He is vast, good, wide, the more your perpetual prayer will bear fruits of fine flavour. One of the dangers is to be cramped by concern over one's iniquity and lack of success, which in a way is to cultivate one's vanity instead of one's love for God.

Next we must find, each in his own way — that which is the reason for having spiritual fathers — a way to allow our soul to be permanently in this breathing prayer. There is the repetition of names: Jesus, or Mary; then there is another way: to keep oneself before God all the time. In itself it is very accessible, and I shall sum it up in two expressions: 'permanence of breath, permanence of God.'

The rhythm of prayer

Good methods form simple recipes. Just as our breathing should be regular, not out of breath, nor slowed down, so it is with prayer; changes are not useful. You breathe; you pray ... you breathe; you pray... and that will become more than yourself.

Breathing is done by inhaling, retaining the air one or a few seconds, then exhaling. It would be good for prayer to adopt the same rhythm. We inhale the divine Name; we hold it, we let it out again. One of the classic examples is hesychasm or the Jesus Prayer:

inhaling: *"Lord Jesus Christ";*
holding;
exhaling: *"Have mercy on me."*

Experience has shown that if we only make the positive movement, or only the negative movement, we do not obtain the normal pulsation of prayer: after receiving the divine names, we must give them back.

In the monastic life, a little gymnastic activity is added: one prostrates oneself, remains prostrated, then rises again. This movement harmonizes the liturgical prayer in a beneficial way: sobriety, solemnity, reception, penitence.

Receiving without effort

Certain missals offer for the morning a category of prayers they call acts of adoration, of faith, of hope, etc... and, for the evening, acts of contrition. Certain Protestant groups and 'boy-scout' instructions advise us, when we rise in the morning, to make a decision to spend the day in some particular way; this is their good deed. This form of prayer is to be completely avoided ... forever! Make no resolutions, and, above all, no essential interior effort.

Obviously, as a person eats, he opens his mouth, takes a fork, chews, then digests. As he breathes, he inhales and exhales the air, and he can learn to breathe properly. But if the physical movements of eating and breathing demand an effort of us, they are harmful. We should receive, assimilate, and not wish to act. I say this for food-prayer and for breath-prayer. Every voluntary decision restricts the possibility of health. Without doubt we can battle against a certain distraction, and, just as we can observe if our chewing is bad, we can watch that we pronounce the words slowly; but this is hygiene, not an effort of will.

I shall give you three images to represent the state of the soul during food-prayer and breath-prayer. Let the soul imitate a *cup*, a receptacle, a 'vessel,' as the Medieval texts say — religious initiations are symbolized by a cup — a cup in which God pours His wine, his grace, His power. Let the soul resemble a *lotus*, a *tulip* which catches the sun's rays or the heavenly dew of the morning. Let the soul become a rose, the heart of which is the sun.

Imagine that your heart is God, radiating in your open being, or, as in that picture which I loved as a child, like Saint Sebastian opening his breast to receive the arrows. When I had a first revelation of the Holy Spirit, He descended on me as a bird coming from the sky and pricked my heart, but my heart was open to receive this wound, this nourishment.

Cup, lotus, tulip, rose, something which opens itself to receive and be fed. Your gestures, your position should not demand of you more effort than that of being well seated at a banquet.

Accept and protect. The Virgin kept in her heart the precious words of her Son.[28]

I have emphasized this behaviour, as many people worry. They think that food prayer depends on an interior activity in which we must become taut, must imagine, desire, fix, and concentrate, instead of protecting, thrusting aside what hinders, and hollowing out the inner cup which God penetrates.

Concentration and intellectual conception are domes which close so that grace cannot spread within them.

PRACTICAL EXERCISES

Breath-prayer

1) Begin practicing breath-prayer: for example five to ten minutes a day, perhaps telling the beads once or twice a day.

2) Unite the prayer to the breathing in two stages:

a) First get the rhythm of your breathing without prayer.
b) Then introduce the prayer into this breathing rhythm.

3) Preferably use the patristic prayer: *"Lord Jesus Christ, Son of God, have mercy on me"*; but another formula can be used if desired.

4) Put yourself into a state of 'openness' — neither in tension nor relaxation.

Questions to ask yourself

1) How many times have I practiced the breath-prayer each day?
2) Have I succeeded in practising it every day for at least one week?
3) What is the rhythm of my breathing?
4) What is my prayer?
5) What is my state of 'openness'?

NOTES

[25] John 6:55.
[26] See Genesis Chap.3, notably 3:22.
[27] The summary of the teachings of Christ in the Gospel of Saint Matthew (Chapters 5-7) contains particularly the Beatitudes and the Lord's Prayer. According to the Gospel description, it is after having been "raised up on the mountain" that Jesus called his disciples close to Him to teach them. See also Luke 6:17-49.
[28] Luke 2:51. See also Luke 2:19.

CHAPTER FIVE

PRAYER, WORK AND REST:
THE RHYTHM OF LIFE

Regularity

I will repeat that, just as the important thing in nourishment is the quantity of food and the regularity with which it is absorbed, food-prayer requires the individual to follow a set of rules that are as far as possible prescribed in advance. When wisely regulated and based on our way of life, this rule of prayer will nourish our soul and make our spirit vigorous. Disorder in life is particularly negative. Unfortunately, our occupations often make our meals irregular — and this is bad — for we do not live in a monastery, which is a 'factory' where prayer is regulated, adjusted, harmonious.

There was a period when everyone was asking me to give him a 'mantra,' in Hindu terms, a personal formula for ceaseless prayer. Ceaseless... for the most part, it was impossible. So I replied then: "Pray only fifteen minutes a day." And when the same person came to me again a month later, this person inevitably admitted having prayed for fifteen minutes on only two or three days during the month. Fifteen minutes each day are not so easy to find in our life. Nevertheless, cost what it may, a certain regularity must be established. Prayer will nourish our spirit in proportion to its regularity. The late Swami Siddeswarananda taught that in order to advance spiritually it is necessary to devote six hours a day to meditation and prayer for five years.[29] Then the first step is passed. He was right. But what are we to do?... We are so restless that a quarter of an hour every day already seems to us very long, although this does not prevent us from wasting hours in useless occupations. It is not the fault of the external situation; it is our own internal instability.

Three times eight hours

What is the classic rule for dividing the day spiritually with the aim of gaining physical, psychic and spiritual balance? The Fathers have said: eight hours of work, eight hours of rest, consisting of sleep, eating, conversation, relaxation, and eight hours of prayer. This is logical and it seems easy. It is the ideal!

We all fall below this ideal. The spirit is always undernourished. We all give ourselves spiritual tuberculosis.

32

Work: that is to say, eight hours of effort, intellectual, manual, business. Intellectual work alone is not always wholesome for equilibrium. It is better to have manual as well as intellectual work. In any case, the intellect consumes too many of our free moments. Whether we look at your life or mine, what do we notice? Much more than eight hours of intellectual work. As for me, I do twelve to fourteen hours; I have not much time left for prayer — apart from liturgy — nor for rest.

Let us not forget that *relaxation* is as useful as prayer and work. Moreover, it does not consist simply of doing nothing. Often our sleep is not a rest because we are so tired that we cannot relax our muscles and our thoughts. When Saint Anthony the Great [30] came out of his desert one day, a prince wanted to make the acquaintance of this exceptional man whose cell filled with flames; he met only a jovial monk discussing hunting, rain, and good weather with a peasant. The noble lord was extremely shocked by the simple manner of this eminent monk. The latter then said to him, *"My friend, if the bowstring is too tight, it breaks. Our Lord granted himself moments of relaxation."*

Most people sleep eight hours, but that is because their life is poorly 'balanced'; six hours of sleep and two hours of real relaxation are enough.

Work, then, is effort; relaxation is absence of effort.

Watchfulness

And the eight hours of *prayer*, are they active or passive? A third term defines them: *watchfulness.* Neither active nor passive, neither effort nor relaxation, neither rest nor free-and-easiness. 'Watchfulness' is the word used by Christ when He said *"Watch and pray."* [31] The spirit is not upheld by a monologue with one's will, one's feeling, or one's intelligence, nor by imposing something on oneself or on others; it is in a state that is simultaneously passive, because it listens, alert to receive, and active because it thrusts distractions aside — standing, present, the string stretched at the right tension so that the divine hand can strike a note from it.

A gradual preparation precedes watchfulness: a place in the day of activity, education for our intelligence, will, and mental capacity. It needs a chance for relaxation as well, and finally a psycho-physical 'chaise-longue' so that the third state of watchfulness can be obtained easily and placed between work and relaxation, a synthesis of the two. The person who is always passive would not attain the active presence, and the person who is always active would be unable to be receptive.

Daily life

In practice, how should we divide these eight hours?

My advice, in spite of everything, is to have the absolute and universal norm before one's eyes, to compare our existence with it, to discern how far we are from it. We do not hope to realize this perfect formula, but it allows us to measure what separates us from the equilibrium we shall try to approach.

Let those who have neither prayer nor rest introduce both into their life. Let experience define their failures more exactly, and then let them endeavour as far as possible to reestablish what is missing and to refill the empty place by diminishing the part that is too inflated.

Alas, the division of our daily life by the two hour interruption at noon[32] is not very suitable. A more complicated arrangement is needed. In the monasteries, prayer is not done in a single stretch. There are hours that are more or less suitable for prayer, more or less suitable for work, and more or less suitable for relaxation. Our modern occupations give us eight hours of work which we cannot alter. And then on top of the eight hours of earning our living, we have more hours of personal work... I do not think that many workers work only eight hours a day. Yet for a human balance, forty hours a week of factory or office work should not be exceeded, as it is necessary to add the personal labour indispensable for the full life of a human being. This was the idea of the socialists, and it was applied between the two wars, but since then it has been eliminated.[33]

Sunday

Three times eight hours, this is the division for the weekday, but what of the seventh day — Sunday — feast days, or vacations ... paid or not? To tell the truth, our modern life has not enough feast days.[34] When the Church had a deep influence on society, holidays were taken much more frequently, but in a different way: not several weeks in succession. Until the French Revolution, all the Christian countries in the world set apart two weeks for Easter, two weeks for Christmas, one or more days for different feasts, etc. Factories did not exist, and as far as possible, work stopped in the workshops.

Now we have the problem of Sunday — and here of course I must make an exception for the priest.

On this day, let us avoid the puritan system, or very catholic, very pious, very 'religious' systems. How does a person belonging to those settings spend Sunday? He prays in the morning; then he eats well, (that no doubt forms part of the prayer); he reads the Bible, takes not too long a walk, yawns his head off, listens to Vespers, and as it is prohibited to work and amusements are also prohibited on the Lord's day, he finds solace in saying spiteful things about other people.

Saint Augustine once remarked that Sundays ought to be skillfully apportioned between relaxation and prayer. The embryo of this relaxation is in the little glasses of wine and the conversations after mass.[35]

I am sometimes asked why do we not stay in the church after Sunday mass to recollect ourselves? If someone wants to concentrate, let him concentrate. But someone who is willing to 'digest' the liturgy, to be nourished by it, should also know how to take rest in a multitude of forms — with beautiful landscapes, the cinema, or in coming together with others. In the primitive Church, these relaxations had such a large place that they became a little noisy and the Fathers were obliged to take measures: the faithful, inspired by the Holy Spirit and the joy of Easter, sometimes crossed the spiritual frontiers of what is useful to the human spirit. It is nonetheless true that relaxation is indispensable.

Vacations

Vacations should also take two forms. Spiritually undernourished as we are during the winter because of our activity, we have an absolute need for complete relaxation and for retreat into prayer. The best solution is a few days of retreat (depending on the individual) — I mean: in isolation — to withdraw even to a monastery, simply to listen to the services, with the least possible preaching. The soul in retreat is nourished by prayer, but not in those organized retreats where one is subjected to indigestible missionaries.

In Spirit and in Truth

I will end by taking up a subject which will be dealt with in the next chapter: our attitude to our own inner life.

Christ said to the Samaritan woman: *"Now God will be worshipped in spirit and in truth."*[36] Certainly spirit and truth indicate the Holy Spirit and Christ ... who called Himself the Truth. One will worship in the Holy Spirit and in Christ; let us apply these words. Our prayer should feed us in spirit and in truth.

What is the meaning of this? Do not look for subtle ways of progressing in the spiritual life. The *spirit*, here, is your heart, your inner inspiration, your impetus, your soul: your religious feeling. The *truth* is your thought, your intelligence, your mental mode.

Prayer, the spiritual nourisher, satisfies the heart and the intelligence as long as both participate in it spontaneously. It is always composed of two elements: the first element will be our love, our desire for God, our penitence before Him; its result is the springing of tears; tears of the vision of limitless Compassion — the gift of tears of joy. The second element refreshes our intelligence by confession and the contemplation of revealed truths, and its inner gaze is ravished by the magnificence of the divine Splendour and its radiation upon the world.

PRACTICAL EXERCISES

On the rhythm of life:

The division of time into three equal parts: watchfulness, work, and relaxation, is impractical under the present conditions of our life; nevertheless we should strive towards this ideal rhythm.
If one of the three parts is absent, for example, watchfulness, try to introduce it for at least half an hour a day, then for an hour, etc.
If one of the parts is weaker, endeavour to increase it and so to come as near as possible to the ideal rhythm.
We should balance:
a) the day
b) the week: ("On the seventh day thou shalt rest")
c) the year: (feasts and vacations)
d) life: (childhood, adult years, old age)

Questions to ask yourself

1) How many hours or minutes have I devoted to prayer, to work, to relaxation?
  each day?
  this week?
  this year?

2) What was the division of my life:
  in the past?
  now?
What are my plans for the future?

NOTES

[29] Swami Siddheswarananda was a member of the Ramakrishna Order and represented it in France. He directed the Vedanta Centre of Paris, where Monseigneur Jean (as Eugraph Kovalevsky) and other members of our Church were invited to speak on the teaching of the Orthodox Church.

[30] An Egyptian hermit of the 3rd and 4th Centuries, one of the greatest of the "Desert Fathers." The *Life of Saint Anthony* by Saint Athanasius of Alexandria (history's first hagiographer) has for long been valued as a model of the ascetic life. Since then, his famous "temptations" have particularly struck the imagination of painters and ascetics. Saint Anthony is regarded as one of the originators of the hesychastic tradition.

[31] Matthew 26:41.

[32] This is usually considerably less in the USA than in France, of course.(Ed.)

[33] This is based on the text of 1958. Since then working hours have been again reduced but are now now increased again for some people.(Ed.)

[34] The word "holidays," of course, once meant "holy days."(Ed.)

[35] As a priest, Eugraph Kovalevsky had the custom, after celebrating the liturgy, of meeting the faithful for a 'jar'. When he became a bishop, he continued this practice.

[36] John 4:23.

CHAPTER SIX

PRAYER "IN SPIRIT AND IN TRUTH"

Effort, relaxation, watchfulness

Effort, relaxation, watchfulness: these are the three attitudes which should make up our day.

I do not think it is useful for us to linger over the study of *effort*. We all know what effort is, and that it is necessary to adjust it to the rhythm of the person who is making it — for some people blossom out in speed, and others by being slow — and we know that agitated effort is harmful.

As to *relaxation*, in our time this is difficult, and it calls for a careful apprenticeship.

Here we would particularly like to consider *watchfulness*, since our modern teaching reserves only a minimal place for this; yet it is intimately linked with prayer.

Medicine speaks of relaxation; many circles, Hindus and naturists for example, speak of relaxation, and there are a number of techniques for acquiring it. Effort too has given rise to an abundant literature, the rationalization of work, for example. We possess pills for sleeping, pills for waking us up, but we have not yet pills for watchfulness. This shows that medicine has not recognized the eminent and legitimate place of prayer, but concerns itself only with man's output and with balancing this with relaxation.

Watchfulness, like all the categories of prayer, appears at first as a paradoxical quality.

Here I shall make a digression in order to accustom your intelligence to approaching the Christian mysteries. What does it mean to think paradoxically? Perfect understanding will not be achieved, but still this is a good exercise. To think paradoxically is to regard opposites not as conflicting elements, but in order to transcend their opposition. The dogma of the two natures in Christ is paradoxical: God-man? Man, although unseparated and inseparable from Divinity, is not confused with It. The dogma of the Trinity is paradoxical: Three and One.

The interior technique of spirituality realizes this grasp of paradoxes.[37] Watchfulness indeed contains a paradoxical element that is both active and passive. If one does not listen, one cannot receive grace, and so the soul is stretched; yet, nevertheless, relaxation is indispensable. But in watchfulness the intelligence and feelings are not suppressed. Let us understand the term watchfulness in a most concrete sense: not to sleep at night, to 'keep watch,' that is to say, to leave the troubled region of the day and enter a zone of tranquility in which nature is at rest yet where at the same time we remain standing and awake.

Watchfulness then includes relaxation, the giving up of all tension, of all activity, and the battle against sleep. We could almost say that the active element is negative, occupied only with throwing off drowsiness, and that the passive element is positive, occupied with creating and maintaining a state of presence.

Dispassion

Hence this technique is explained by a strange word which the Fathers used: *apatheia*. This term has no sense of apathy, nor of indifference. *Apatheia* is one of the instruments given us by our watchfulness. It renews the external impressions which permit us to remain 'present'. It is like a man who listens attentively. Someone who speaks is in action, but someone who listens with attention is not, properly speaking, active; yet he is so in the sense that he is actively attentive.

Before and during prayer, the work consists in struggling to keep this state of watchfulness: an absence of sleep and an absence of tension. This is expressed in the following manner: suddenly a word of the prayer strikes you, or a revelation is disclosed to you, or your heart burns with love, with penitence. You feel like a cup open to grace. Give attention! Accept this grace without settling yourself into it. On the other hand, even if your prayer is impeded by incapacity, by distraction, because your soul is heavy, maintain your effort and pray just the same. *"Watch and pray, that ye enter not into temptation."* [38] Temptation arises precisely when we are not watchful.

This vigilance will nourish us spiritually — provided that during our life it is blended with complete relaxation and with work: a harmony of letting go and of work on yourself and with others. Let your time borrow its double face from watchfulness.

Deepening of breath prayer

Let us go back to breath-prayer and look at it more deeply.

Side by side with the food-prayer, which is liturgical prayer, lives the breath-prayer. Its very nature makes it permanent, for the person who does not breathe dies. As we have shown in the preceding chapters, food prayer develops, stops, takes up again, while breathing prayer should not stop. The spirit attains total health when the person prays without ceasing, in conformity with his breathing and analogous to it.

Christ teaches that the Father should be worshipped *"in spirit and in truth."* [39] The first lesson of this phrase is that we must pray to the Father in the Holy Spirit through the Son: 'spirit' designates the Holy Spirit, and 'truth' the Son. But the immediate meaning, which proceeds from this as if it were a reflection of it, is that breathing prayer has two characters: spirit and truth.

It presents itself in two different forms: without words, with words; without words before words, in silence after words.

I will explain myself: prayer without words 'before' is unceasing; the soul 'walks before God,' as the Bible says. This is to live and act before God. We find that a multitude of obstacles prevent us from living permanently on this level.

So we make use of the perpetual prayer that is called a 'mantra' by the Hindus. Its formulae are many; the Orthodox teaching refers to one, principally — and we have already spoken of it — *"Lord Jesus Christ, Son of God, have mercy on me."* This form, the most frequently adopted, the best loved, the most professed, is not unique. *"Kyrie eleison,"* "Lord, have mercy" is a perpetual prayer which comes to us from the early Church. Many others can exist.

Brevity

Brevity, like breathing, is the external character of these formulae. It is not a banquet.

I would say in passing that a number of people claim that the Eastern services last too long. It is a question of what one is used to; did not wedding banquets in Normandy last five, six hours and more? Our physical stomach and our spiritual stomach have become smaller! The East has not been able to accustom itself to celebrating services the way one eats a sandwich on the counter. The French Churches of the time of the Franks still had very long services.

Brevity is like breathing. Perpetual prayer will then begin with the repetition of a short phrase that is always the same. This phrase prepares the way for prayer without words, in which our nature becomes a prayer which *"flows from our heart"* and regulates its breathing.

Let us recapitulate. Breathing prayer begins with an attitude: to walk with God; it is realized in perpetual prayer which transforms our whole being, to end in prayer without words, where the person is prayer, and breathes it with full lungs. This is the tradition of Seth, the third son of Adam, who was the first to call on the Name of the Lord.[40]

Spirit and heart

Yesterday I had a striking example of prayer based solely on the spirit. The person in question was a Christian with a hinduizing tendency, living on prayer and on long, very long meditations which fed his feeling. (I must emphasize that the nourishing prayer of the heart places the person between the hands of God; he listens to the divine will; he endeavours to accomplish it; he is laid hold of by Him; he enlightens others and his path is noble.) I thought then for a long time that this man would some day notice the deficiency of this prayer that was based solely on feeling and listening to the divine will. This is what happened. With simplicity he observed that he was losing his foothold on the ground as well as the capacity to act by himself, that his influence, instead of bringing solutions to others' difficulties, offended them, annoyed them, let us say the word: he lacked tact. Certainly he often spoke the truth, but his words lacked calm analysis and discernment ...not to speak of his own affairs, which were in a bad way. Now you will say to me: cannot a praying person live as a recluse? My friends, even the life of a recluse needs to be organized. This man had wanted to centre his prayer on feeling, without strengthening his intelligence. By good fortune he had understood; but he said to me sadly: "If I change, I shall lose this intense prayer, this presence, this union!" — "Yes," I replied, "you will lose them temporarily, to find them again later on."

As we seek for our heart to become warm, for obedience to God, for reception of grace, it is indispensable to avoid the thought which distinguishes and analyzes. The only thought which does not run counter to the heart is that of identification with God, that of union. All that is dual, multiple, variegated, immediately prevents the heart from being available, from being in God's hands, from receiving his light. The Hindu conception: *"I am God,"* in the sense that 'I' am confused with Him, that 'I' in reality do not exist, that all is God, is not a truth but a thought at the service of the heart's experience, because the heart demands perfect unity. This instrumental conception, in the service of the heart, leads experimentally to the loss of contact with the real, with the world, and even with oneself. And this is why Christ teaches us to pray "in spirit and *in truth.*"

"Lord Jesus Christ, Son of God, have mercy on me"

Now we will analyze an example of unceasing prayer, the most classical: *"Lord Jesus Christ, Son of God, have mercy on me."*[41]

It is divided into two parts: *"Lord Jesus Christ, Son of God"* and *"have mercy on me."* These two parts are different. The first confesses and addresses itself to our intelligence; we 'feel' it differently; it is the truth. *"Have mercy on me"* strikes our heart; we understand the necessity of the Mercy of God. This second part is subjective, while the beginning is objective.

If it is composed only of the name of Jesus, the Jesus Prayer cannot satisfy Christ's condition for prayer, that it be *in spirit and in truth.* The reason is psychological: the last centuries have surrounded the name of Jesus with an

41

emotional atmosphere. The person who pronounces it unceasingly can quickly feel warmth of heart, but his intelligence will not be sustained, (the name 'Jesus Christ' is now a stranger to spontaneous feeling). At least at first, the characteristic of the nourishment of the intelligence is always to belong to something which has no direct, immediate connection with us — we could use the term 'objective' — but which is like the rock upon which the Church is built, a stable rock, a solid rock cementing the intelligence to the heart. Our Lord wants our unceasing prayer to catch the divine life as if with pincers, pincers with two faces.

The prayer that is capable of expanding our lungs and filling them with health contains at the same time an element of truth, of revelation, and one that subjectively moves our soul. Every prayer, even momentary, must have both, or it will be deficient. Without that, we shall not breathe the fresh air of God.

One principle of unceasing prayer which we should take account of is that it is given by heaven, or by the spiritual father. We have different ones, among others the admirable prayer of Saint Joannicus: *"The Father is my hope; the Son is my protection; my shield is the Holy Spirit."* You see, the action strikes the heart, but the divine names strike our intelligence. This prayer is Trinitarian in three stages.

As for prayer linked to the breath, the classic formula is this: when inhaling we confess and serve our intelligence; when exhaling we give to our heart.

Is it not said these days that we should *"receive the truth"* and *"give the spirit."* "He who receives the truth," as Christ says in His sermon on the mount, builds his house on a solid foundation; one who only receives inspiration will live in a house without foundations. Inspiration leads one to the heights, but also to falls.

I have met many souls coming from Roman or Hinduizing atmospheres, (I am not speaking of actual Hindus, whose situation is very different). Both of these worlds are interested in unceasing prayer, and they have confided to me that the prayer *"Lord Jesus Christ, have mercy on me"* said nothing' to them, that it seemed to them without flavour, brought them no quick experience in which the heart burns, in which the mind is pierced with light. What does this mean? That our intelligence is almost no longer fed by Christian truth. As Henri Petit writes in his book *The Honour of God: "All the French live richly from the point of view of money, but have been accustomed from childhood to live poorly from the point of view of the spirit."* Hindus nourish their intelligence abundantly by their metaphysics, while Christians are left hungry because the Christian revelation no longer forms the basis of their spiritual meal.

PRACTICAL EXERCISES

Elements of the breath-prayer.

To be authentic, breath prayer:
— in inhaling: should confess the revealed Truth — which transcends our subjective conception
— in holding the breath: should hold to the spirit in silence
— in exhaling: should formulate a request conforming to our intimate being

Example:
— inhaling: *Lord Jesus Christ* (revealed Truth)
— silence...
— exhaling: *Have mercy on me!* (Conforming to my intimate being)
or, add to the request: *have mercy on me! a sinner.*

Questions to ask yourself

1)   In practicing the breath-prayer, have I in inhaling let the revealed Truth inform my intelligence, or am I left with my own reasonings?
2)   Have I succeeded in keeping my spirit in silence?
3)   In exhaling, have I placed my trust solely in the divine Mercy, or have I clung to my own free will?

NOTES

[37] This means, using paradoxes or *antinomies* to think about things in a broader way, is a fundamental approach in Orthodox Russian thought. (Ed.)

[38] Matthew 26:41.

[39] John. 4:23.

[40] See. Genesis 4:26 : *"Seth was also a son and called by the name of Enoch. It was thus that he began to call on the name of the Lord."* In the King James Bible the translation suggests that Enoch was the son of Seth. (Ed.)

[41] We will notice that the formula commented on by the author is shorter than that most commonly used: *"Lord Jesus Christ, Son of God, have mercy on me, a sinner."*

CHAPTER SEVEN

THE STEPS TO UNCEASING PRAYER

The three steps of prayer

A confessed truth does not immediately resonate in the soul, and it is easier for us to catch the cosmic rhythm than the divine Thought. So the Fathers tell us we that must foresee as inevitable several preliminary periods of time that make it possible to end up in unceasing prayer. They are:

> the mechanical period
> the mental period
> the heart period

During the mechanical period the person who prays applies himself to say the prayer regularly (a hundred times, a thousand times ... a quarter of an hour, a half hour or an hour ... per day). He can reserve definite times for this prayer, or use moments available during manual work, when travelling, etc... This prayer continues without the words being held firmly by the spirit. The only preoccupation of the one who prays will be not to fail in the decision taken, whether it is so many repetitions or so many hours each day.

In mental prayer, the person praying assimilates the words of the prayer. He pronounces them consciously, so that they should not simply be 'close' to his thought, but should be 'his' thought. This second step is already so effective that the soul begins completely to get rid of enemy number one of his spiritual health: which is the air poisoned by useless thoughts, that partially unconscious climate in which a person is thought by his thoughts.

As well as unceasing prayer, there exist excellent methods for starting prayer by thinking in words. The word is chosen, then articulated aloud, then it is introduced into the mind. Before psychoanalysis was born, the ancients were already applying this kind of therapy to individuals who were violently tormented by serious problems. They made them trace the name of an object placed before them in large writing at a very slow rhythm: lamp, for example. If at the end of a certain time the patients succeeded in identifying themselves for one second with the thought of the lamp, they could be healed, coming out of this sickness in which the multitude of thoughts — friendly or beastly — were jostling and smothering like the rush-hour crowd on the underground. This method, as old as the world, this traditional culture (tradition equals transmission) rests on repetition.

The third step is definitive. The person praying brings his prayer down into his heart so that it can be kindled, can take fire there, and can then flow without words: *"He who believes on me ... rivers of living water* (unceasing prayer) *will flow from his belly."* [42]

Mechanical prayer

A person who, on the advice of his spiritual father, had recently undertaken to practice the Jesus Prayer for half an hour a day — in spite of his many occupations — confided to me that despite the distraction and wandering of thought, the 'mechanical' practice of the prayer, as it penetrated his soul, had brought him tranquility; the restlessness and over-nervousness had been calmed, and the tyrannical pressure of his ailing psyche was losing its power. Without having acquired a deep peace, he said that at least he was no longer in disarray and that a stable point had formed in his soul. This experience can be realized by everyone. We need only to anchor ourselves in this practice regularly and without interruption.

The 'mechanical' step, of course, does not transform the interior man, for it remains external to consciousness. But in spite of its secondary character, it is nevertheless not without virtues: the goodwill of prayer has a moral value, and the powerful and objective influence of the sacred words and the divine names has a divine value.

The fact of qualifying this step as 'mechanical' does not at all signify that we automatically have the power to enclose the energy of the name of Jesus. This formidable energy is given to man only as much as he can bear it. One could attribute the term 'volitional' to this step, but we prefer 'mechanical' in order to avoid the argument about 'merits'.

Spiritual law and moral law: 'Merits'

In fact, in making it a strict rule to repeat the prayer, the free will of the person praying is exposed to the danger of a feeling of 'merit' and reward. Certainly God appreciates human effort. He is not ungrateful: *"for a sou, He is eager to give back a thousand francs,"* as a monk said. A sacrifice that is minimal for Him is received in heaven with joy. But although He takes account of the least movement of goodwill, although He receives it as a gift of great price, that does not grant us the right to claim something in return, nor the impression that God has no claim on us. We will always be 100% in his debt.

The conception of 'merits' hardens the soul and immobilizes its progress. Our heart ceases to be hungry for salvation, our 'ego' is inflated, and the divine

45

'I' is expelled from our spirit. The *Philokalia* ('love of the beautiful'), an encyclopaedia of the masters of the spiritual life from the first to the eighteenth centuries,[43] a particularly precious book for the technique of prayer, makes no use of this term.

We do not want to discard this word from our vocabulary; its place there is legitimate, but we wish to underline that in the interior work of man, and for the effectiveness of prayer, it is essential to avoid it. When we say that an individual who has suffered on earth 'deserves Paradise,' we do not make a mistake, but if we assert: "I have earned Paradise and grace," we commit a fault with respect to our soul, which has been entrusted to us. Here is revealed a law which is little understood, which even seems unjust and illogical: to adorn oneself with merit is harmful, to pour merits upon others is excellent. Goodwill, or personal effort, incontestable as their value is, cannot serve as a medium of exchange.

The spiritual law differs from the moral law without contradicting it; it transcends it and even alters the problems. Thus actions or states which are morally indifferent or neutral are sometimes spiritually fatal.

The unconscious and subconscious provoke involuntary acts for which man is not responsible on the moral plane — and it is the same for the superconscious (the state of grace) — whereas on the spiritual plane it is necessary to take these acts into consideration. So it is necessary to outwit them, to purify the unconscious or subconscious, which can cunningly undermine us. Without superconsciousness, or a state of grace (a consciousness enlightened by God), there is no spiritual evolution.

Effectiveness of mechanical prayer

I come back once more to the virtue of the divine names, even when they are pronounced with neither intention nor conviction. As long as our heart and intelligence are still outside God, we cannot truly feel grace as the mechanism of the prayer unfolds. It is only after turning all our capacities towards Him, without sharing them with this world, that we perceive His light.

Still let us not despise mechanical prayer; let us accept the rosaries; even if this first step falsely appears to some people as final and definitive, it is neither useless nor unfruitful. I was witness to the Jesus Prayer recited regularly in a subdued tone in half-darkness for about an hour. I do not believe that those praying had passed the first step, for they pronounced the prayer at the tip of their lips, and so fast that it was impossible for them to grasp the holy words with their thought ... and yet, behold: this hour of prayer released a pacifying power not only on those present but on the place itself, obliterating the phantoms of the psyche and the disturbing shadows, exhaling the tranquility of the dawn, invisible but quietly palpable to the soul.

Mental prayer

The second step, that of 'mental' prayer, must be described exactly. Certainly I have already indicated the essential, but as modern man has lost direct knowledge and has made his intellectual and emotional reflexes extremely complicated, it is good to try to define it.

It is not enough to understand, to comment on it, to meditate on it, to feel it — it is a question of consciously connecting with the words, of 'seeing' them with the intelligence.

The wisdom of Zen is being propagated in our time in the West; those who know it will understand us more easily. On the practical level, this Asiatic wisdom teaches us to consider things as they are: a stick is a stick. Some physicians use this for restoring mental and psychic balance: they require the consenting patient not to isolate himself in his closed world any longer, but to go out towards objects by means of simple sensations (to listen to the sound, simply as it is; to look at colours just as they are, etc.) Spiritually we are all sick, in a more or less clinical state; we are all sinners; we are all in sin.

Let us take as an example the five words of the classic Jesus Prayer: *"Lord Jesus Christ, have mercy on me,"* (In the old languages, Greek, Latin, Slavonic, *"have mercy"* is only one word, the fourth, and *"on me"* is the fifth.)

Saint Paul wrote: *"I would rather speak five words that consciously mean something than ten thousand words in distraction."* [44]

When we say: *"Lord,"* we must register the fact that we have said *"Lord,"* and not *"Jesus,"* or *"Christ,"* or *"have mercy,"* or *"on me"*; and when we pronounce: *"Jesus,"* that we have not said *"Lord,"* or *"Christ,"* etc. When we continue: *"have mercy,"* we must be aware that we are not asking Him to *"love me,"* or *"purify me,"* and when we end *"on me,"* we must distinguish that it is not *"on you"* or *"on us."*

Strike the word with the mind in such a way that direct contact is established between the thought and the word, without parasites on the way, nor sliding towards other words or analogous ideas. *Be attentive* to the prayer. The Virgin was fully 'attentive,' keeping the words in her heart, stripped of reflexes and reflections. She had *integrity.*

This stage of mental prayer enlightens our being, makes us pass from the external to the internal, and guides us towards the threshold of the temple of the Holy Spirit built within us. Our view of the external world and ourselves is deepened and 'made more exact.' Relations with those who use mental prayer are salutary. They exhale intelligence and prudence; they no longer judge their neighbours because their thought is full of the divine name and their soul is cultivated by the supplication: *"Have mercy on me."* A sense of proportion, lucidity and goodwill germinates in their heart — but those who rush into the Jesus Prayer with the desire to direct others, instead of fleeing from human commerce in order to be only with Jesus, face a spiritual danger. Listen well: he who thinks that he alone is in need of being saved is on the path of the spirit; he who believes that he can save others is on the path of illusion; he is close to spiritual madness.

Repeat and go deeper

If you experience too many difficulties to enter mental prayer, two exercises will be helpful:

Repeat each word several times for a certain period of time: *Lord Jesus, Jesus — have mercy, have mercy — on me, on me ...* Impress, confirm, drive in, fasten the word in our brain.

Go deeper into the theological value of each of these repeated words, for example: *Lord* is the name which confesses the divinity of Christ, *Jesus* confesses His humanity. The Name: JESUS [45] is a formidable power against the infernal powers and the sweet delight of just souls.

These two exercises: to repeat, and to deepen, are not given to replace prayer, but to sustain it. Mental prayer is only the royal door to the heart sanctuary, for it is the pure heart — and not the intelligence — that sees God in His Light: *"Blessed are the pure in heart, for they shall see God."* [46]

And so we reach the last step.

Prayer of the heart

This third step should be envisaged in two aspects: human effort, and with it, the action of the uncreated energy of the Trinity. This action plants the mental prayer in our heart. The monk bends and searches his heart. Christ, the writers of the primitive Church tell us, often had His head bent over his chest, not from sorrow or dejection, but from the interiorization of His human nature, always united through His human body to His divine nature. In Him, the man obeyed and listened to God; the Son obeyed and listened to His Father.

Here we should proceed to the anatomy of the human body. That is not possible for us, so let us simply say that the centre, the core of our body — the heart in the chest — is that part least deeply felt by us. Our head is continually at work; our lower organs are quickly kindled. The organ of the heart is almost forgotten. When passions catch light in it, remember Christ's words: *"For out of the heart proceed evil thoughts: murders, adulteries, fornications, thefts, perjury, false witness, blasphemies"*; [47] they propagate through our tissues in two directions: downwards and upwards, like a tepid humidity. At the opposite pole to the heart, they are only caricatures of the divine Resemblance seated in our heart.

The pure heart is acquired, is conquered, by ascetic purification of the lower, and by the descent of the higher into the heart. Someone who bends towards the heart in prayer will progressively establish the prayer in this holy centre, will wrap the 'word' of the prayer within himself, hide the treasure there, will enter spiritually into the private chamber until the day when God Himself, by His grace and uncreated energy, renews him, brings the permanent prayer to flower, without words, without a break, rushing like a brook, burning like a sanctuary-lamp, refreshing, warming, perfuming, illuminating his being.

But I fear to go too far. Let us go forward with courage, step by step, with no perilous leaps over the abysses. Let us advance in our spiritual ascent with confidence and prudence

PRACTICAL EXERCISES

The three steps of breath-prayer.

Mechanical: accustom yourself to pronounce the words of the prayer distinctly and without haste.

Mental: grasp each word of the prayer in your mind so that it may become present to the vision of our intelligence.

Of the Heart: bend the face and the spirit towards the chest, the centre of our being, and wait patiently for the spontaneous emergence of the prayer.

Questions to ask yourself

1) Am I on the 'mechanical' step?
2) Are the words of the prayer grasped by my *mind*; are they present to the awareness of my intelligence?
3) Have I succeeded in bending my face and my spirit to my chest, the intimate centre of my being?

NOTES

[42] John. 7:38.

[43] *Philokalia* (shortened title): compiled by Saint Macarius of Corinth (an ancient bishop who became a hermit) and Saint Nicodemus the Hagiorite of the Holy Mountain (a monk of Mount Athos, from which his name) and published in Venice in 1782, based on the writings of thirty or so contemplative authors since the first centuries of Christian monasticism up to the time of the reaction against medieval scholasticism and the neo-paganism of the Renaissance. Its translation in 1793 into Slavonic, the liturgical language used in the Slavic countries, was an enormous success and in those countries, particularly in Russia, it stimulated hesychasm, that is, traditional Orthodox mysticism based on the practice of the "Prayer of the name of Jesus," also known as "prayer of the heart." The *Philokalia* has been described as "the sum of the prayer of Jesus" : see *The Prayer of Jesus*, by a monk of the Eastern Church. Three of five volumes have been translated from Greek into English and published by Faber and Faber as *The Philokalia, the complete text.* For an example of its spiritual repercussions in Russia, see one of the several translations of *The Way of the Pilgrim.*

[44] I Corinthians 14:9. But it is less clearly put in the King James Version.

[45] You will find the essential texts in the Liturgy service for the first of January.

[46] Matthew 5:8.

[47] Matthew 15:19.

CHAPTER EIGHT

GOD — 'I'— THE EXTERNAL WORLD
THE DESIRE FOR GOD

"Make me wish whatever you will"

We have spoken about repeating a short prayer without stopping, but can we always do this? We can pray in the train, on the bus, when we are washing the vegetables, perhaps even while we are talking. But when it is a matter of solving a material, practical, intellectual or metaphysical problem, the spirit hardens so that there are moments when it is difficult for the soul to pray, and it is hardly possible to pray while sleeping.

Nevertheless, without unceasing prayer the spirit does not breathe, even if it is fed. Christians who do not have this mode of prayer are half-dead. How can we get out of this impasse?

Let us not be discouraged; let us accept that the present state of our spirit is that of someone half-alive, a sleepwalker. Indeed, beyond unceasing prayer there is silhouetted a realm of *presence* united to the breath of God, in Whom words fall away ... How can we penetrate this?

Here we face a paradox. On the one hand, God knows what He wants: let us assume, for example, that He wants us to be perfect or holy (and He does); yet on the other hand He does not help us to accomplish what He wants. Let us take an image: an employer orders his employee to write a letter and take it to the post, and the latter answers: *"I beg you, with your thought and your strength, help me to post this letter;"* that seems logically ridiculous, but it is exactly like that in the spiritual life. To implore God: *"Make me want what You will, help me to do Your will."*

Waking the filial desire for God

And then another possibility appears, one which can replace unceasing prayer, one that can be acquired quite quickly and can in fact become the unceasing prayer of our life. This consists in the awakening, in the creation in us of the ardent, filial desire for God. We do not have this desire, or so little! Our indifferent heart lives on other things. How can we make this fervent desire, this cry, spring up in us? In one second it can be created for our whole life, either as a result of a period of prayer, or revealing itself in a retreat: every case is individual. The Apostle Paul says of the Holy Spirit that He cries in our souls: *"Abba, Father!"*

"And if the Spirit of Him who raised Jesus from the dead is living in you; then He who raised Jesus from the dead is living in you, then He who raised Jesus from the dead will give life to your own mortal bodies through His Spirit living in you. So, my brothers, there is no necessity for us to obey our unspiritual selves or to live unspiritual lives. If you live in that way, you are doomed to die; but if by the Spirit you put an end to the misdeeds of the body, you will live. Everyone moved by the Spirit is a son of God. The spirit you received is not the spirit of slaves bringing fear into your lives again; it is the spirit of sons, and it makes us cry out, 'Abba! Father!' The Spirit Himself gives testimony to our spirit that we are children of God. So, if we are children of God, we are His heirs: heirs of God and co-heirs with Christ; if we always suffer with Him, in the end we will be glorified with Him."[48]
Experimentally, not merely ontologically, we are one with the Spirit. It is this that makes us sons of God; it is He who cries in us, with our spirit: "Abba. Father!" More than this, Saint Paul adds that we suffer with Christ so as to share his glory, which identifies us inwardly with Christ: *"I no longer live, but Christ lives in me"*[49] This is the grace or acquisition of the Holy Spirit.

If we can touch the goal by means of a long technique or by some method of prayer, we can attain it by grace. Go into prayer so that the Spirit may descend palpably in us, may mingle with our spirit, mix with it, make a oneness with us in a certain way, so that He Himself prays in us. If we have not the strength to breathe God, let the Spirit of God breathe God in us. Let the Spirit carry our spirit.

How shall we proceed so that the Spirit may come into us in a way which we can deeply feel? What can we do so that our spirit, caught up by the Spirit, will cry, *"Abba! Father!"*, so that the Holy Spirit will no longer manifest itself as light, but as prayer (for this is one of the manifestations of his acquisition)? If we have the gift; the problem is solved, otherwise, what shall we do to possess it? The Apostle Paul affirms: *"You are sons of God, and the Spirit cries in you: 'Abba! Father!"* It is as these children that we cry: *"Abba! Father!"*

Can we begin by asking God: *"Make us love You?"* I do not think that this supplication would be enough, for our heart is not yet open. This prayer is good; nevertheless, even if it is ardent, it cannot prepare us for the idea that we do not truly love. We shall examine our soul to discover whether we love or not; our love for God will perhaps be only a projection, an imagination, a mental conception which is voluntary, sentimental, an abstract structure.. We will cry: *"I love You!"* But our heart will remain indifferent.

"Love Thyself, Thyself in me!"

Let us now add a second part to our prayer; let us follow the sighs of our heart: *"Make us love Thee, O God!"* by: *"Lord, as I do not love Thee, love Thyself, Thyself in me!"* This second part will be the point of our soul, the most difficult to grasp, like a needle plunged in the divine fire and bearing the divine spark.

The work of the spiritual life, according to the thought of Saint Gregory the Theologian, is to touch this geometrical spot that is divinely fed: this point, as Meister Eckhart calls it.

This prayer formula: *"Love Thou Thyself in me!"* without our even having to say "with my spirit," bears with it our essential Self. Intellectually it borders on heresy, because God claims our love and feels no need to be loved by Himself. And yet here we find absolute, experimental efficacy. The Apostle Paul teaches that the Spirit, when it is present in us, is almost united with our spirit. If the Holy Spirit is the right hand raised towards the Father, and our spirit is the left hand, join one to the other; then the right hand will pull, and the left will follow.

This prayer of a double love, performed with watchfulness, transforms and kindles the heart in such a manner that it allows it — without repeated prayer — to be busy with the most distracting occupations without ceasing to breathe God. It brings almost the same results; I say 'almost', because the body is not yet in harmony with the heart. It saves our spirit, but the psyche and the body will be looking for something; they will still loiter around the point of our 'I', the divine spark. The total person will not yet be ... I shall say: saved; but the central point will feel attracted and inspired by God.

"Where your treasure is, there will your heart be also"

I have frequently used the term *"desire."* This is a great problem! The Gospel for Ash Wednesday tells us: *"Where your treasure is, there will your heart be also."* [50] Now we desire the treasure. Do you know that a very old spiritual method is not to exterminate one's desire, even though it is evil? Every desire is moved by a vibration of life: turn it onto another path.

We can never emphasize this point too much: man contemplates; man loves, and that is good; nevertheless, he only goes forward if his desire is kneaded, is moulded. If he does not shape it, other desires will come upon him.

A person without desire is asleep. Saint Dionysius the Areopagite teaches that God introduced desire into the primordial chaos ... what one could call the humidity of the world, the aspiration towards being, the impulse towards God. When the Psalms sing: *"I have sought thee from the dawn,"* [51] they sing of the desire for God. In truth, the depth of love is not enjoyment but a call for presence. So do not despise desire, but orient it towards God.

The Gospel tells us that Christ healed sickness by his divine power and, it adds later on, by compassion for the sick. Compassion towards the sick person arouses in the latter a desire to be healed, and the divine power grants it.

Without compassion, you will not go to meet desire, and without desire, even if you are all-powerful, you will not act.

Here we touch the higher world: *"God, love Thou Thyself in me"*; and the human world, the cultivation of the desire: *"I groan for Thee."* The heart beats with hope, with suffering, with inner need, with petition, it "groans for God." The soul suffers, and it is then that the prayer: *"Love Thou Thyself in me, act Thou,"* does not rebound as from a stone, but enters the flesh. We cry out with the Prophet Ezekiel: *"The heart of stone has become a heart of flesh."* And this heart of flesh — no external circumstance will be able to stop its groaning towards God.

To live Christ

Our eighth chapter ends the first part of the teaching on the technique of prayer.

After having presented several paths and indicated narrow ways leading through prayer to union with God, and through purification of our being to the restoration of man to his first beauty, we advise our readers to apply to themselves, without haste or delay, the 'recipes' which we have given.

Carried out each day, the assimilation of a phrase from the Bible or the spiritual Fathers will strengthen and enrich the reasonable heart.

We have given advice not in the form of a literary work, but of a free conversation, in order to avoid the lure of rational structures and to make the reader touch it existentially, to 'eat' and breathe God. It will — we hope — help in their early steps those who desire to live Christ, and not to be Christians only in name.

The absolute objectivity of God

The modern conception of the world is false at its basis. The apprentice in prayer will have to actively renounce the heresy of our century if he wants the yoke of prayer to become light and the burden of watchfulness to become sweet.

In effect, we have become accustomed to consider that what is objective is outside us and that, on the contrary, our inner life is specifically subjective. This form of thought has been transformed into evidence, into an undisputable certainty. Thus, those who oppose scientific and technical progress imagine that they should desperately defend the subjectivity of the inner life, paradoxically joining themselves with Lenin, for whom religion is a 'private affair'. Twentieth century man believes in general that science, nature, and matter are objective, and that religion and the inner life are subjective. Then, in reaction to this, others proclaim that all objectivity is an evil which is crushing humanity.

Are we faced with a dualism from which there is no way out: in which spirit, inner life, and subjectivity are good and matter, the exterior, and objectivity are bad?

Christian dogma affirms that the divine reality — God within us — is objective, that it is not simply a product of our conviction, of our choice, of our imagination, of our faith, of our thought or our effort; no, the divine reality is transcendently objective to all subjectivity, although it is really present within us. If the God we seek is the product of our 'I', we become idealists, spiritualists, and we are no longer Christians.

God-within-us should be conquered as the peak of a high mountain. The technique of prayer is an outfitting for mountaineering. The ropes, the ice-axes, the spiked shoes, the climbing practices, our resistance to the purity of the air, to fatigue, to cold, to hunger, all are indispensable if we are to reach the summit, which remains objective to all that. The summit was, is, and shall be ... even if no mountain climber undertakes to get there. So it is with the objective God within us.

We should drive in, impress into our head that God is more, much more, incomparably more objective than the visible world. The objectivity of the outer world is relative; we can change it. Nothing can change God.

Certainly God is not an object, a thing, an impersonal energy, nor is He even 'a being': He is He Who is; He is the Subject, Tri-Hypostatic (Three-Personal), whence the necessity of prayer, of dialogue, but to be the Subject does not mean that He is to be confused with our individuality. Transcendent in His nature, He is immanent in His energy. Just as we cannot impose our law on created nature, but can only scrutinize and apply its own laws for our needs, in the same way — in an incommensurably absolute way — we cannot impose our law on God. This evidence is no evidence recognised by the logic of modern man: he spends his time constructing his own God!

Face to face with God

Let us reject this artificial dualism: *spirit-subjectivity* and *matter-objectivity*. Let us postulate the axiom that God, in Himself or in us, is total objectivity. Let us place our psycho-spiritual being, variable, unstable, and so very complex, in the face of this objective peak: God in us; and let us contemplate this with the eye of our heart, yet without renouncing the outward gaze at nature with our eyes.

We will obtain the following outline:

God	absolute objectivity
me	subjectivity and the
external world	relative objectivity

Therefore, from another point of view:

God	the centre
the outer world	the periphery
me	the movement of the rays

The present unbalance is a result of the fact that, outside and within us, the absolute objectivity has disappeared from our consciousness. So those who are intoxicated by technical success suddenly notice that human values have been trampled on, while the others, the defenders of the spiritual life, no longer possess the effective support needed to combat the robot. God, the absolute objectivity, has disappeared.

In the next chapters we shall take up the prayer of God addressed to God, the absolute objectivity within us: the prayer of Christ, the 'Lord's Prayer.'

PRACTICAL EXERCISES

Revision

1) Let us note what we have accomplished and what we have not accomplished.

2) Have we really distinguished the Spirit of God in us from own spirit?

3) Have we truly founded our progress on Him, or have we founded it on ourselves: on our will, thought, feeling, our state of soul ... on attachment?

NOTES

[48] Romans 8:11-17.
[49] Galatians 2:20.
[50] Matthew 6:21.
[51] Wrongly attributed to Psalm 63, although there are similar passages in several other Psalms.

PART TWO
THE LORD'S PRAYER

CHAPTER NINE

THE DUAL NATURE OF HOLY SCRIPTURE

The *Our Father* is the prayer of prayers, the most direct, and the most difficult.

Origen subtly defined the dual nature of Holy Scripture: on the one hand it is simple and direct, yet on the other hand it baffles our understanding. It reminds us of the lion or that little creature, the cat; with an indifferent air, a far-away look, they suddenly turn and seize their prey. Suddenly a word in the holy books strikes you, a word that is simple and direct; or an image strikes you - like that of the Father welcoming his prodigal son [52] - then, two lines further on, you are struck by the opposite: the meaning of a word, of a sentence, of an image, will evade you altogether; you are even irritated by it; certain passages are mute and they may remain so for centuries.

Let us suppose for a moment that Holy Scripture, or the spiritual teaching of a prayer such as the Lord's Prayer, reveals itself to us fully, that everything in it is easy, with nothing to discuss: then what will happen to the human soul? It will settle into this understanding as into an armchair - and death occurs precisely when man finds comfort.

There is a profound difference between inner serenity and the pseudo-peace of the person who knows everything, who has the key to the mysteries in his pocket. A friend of my youth once commented on this: two deaths await the human body, he said; one, which we know and record, is the separation of the body and the soul; the other takes place, for a large number of people, between the ages of twenty-five and thirty-five. Before that age we are restless, isolated; we are seeking, vibrating; our gaze is charged with life. Marriage comes; the person we marry is charming or disagreeable; we have a certain baggage of acquaintances, enough fatigue that we no longer think, enough religious negligence that we no longer pray, and towards the age of thirty our gaze is deadened; we have become a complete woman or man, a person of property with his visiting cards. We are established. We have found our 'armchair' of the psyche, and truly this is death. The enigmatic, the things that trouble us in life, have been put tidily into a drawer, separated from existence. Metaphysics? That is for the theologian. The inner life? That belongs to psychiatrists and priests. Saint Isaac the Syrian calls this state *quietude*, or the death of the soul.

What happens then? The body continues to function, it undergoes psychic, mechanical reactions in the manner of Pavlov's celebrated experiments. Sometimes a catastrophe explodes, which could awaken this person, but in general he comes to rest and accepts that he 'should' resign himself. The unknown, the unexpected, the painful move away. And as we avoid this element which makes us each instant evolve simultaneously in knowledge and ignorance, in searching and acquiring knowledge — are not cold and heat necessary to make a locomotive function? — as we neutralize these two poles, we come to a halt. Although Christians could always be 'awakened', many, after the age of thirty, are misfits in the spiritual life, only their psycho-physical organism continues to function.

The goal of Holy Scripture and of spiritual teaching is precisely life, the progress and evolution of the soul. This is the reason why they take on a double aspect: direct elements which surprise us so greatly that they become identified with our being, and elements which are incomprehensible and baffling. Certain passages provoke violent reactions, not only in the course of a man's existence, but through the centuries. The parable is a popular way of teaching; nevertheless the parable of the unjust Steward[53] whose behaviour proves more or less justified plunges us into astonishment, and likewise Christ's words *"Do not think that I have come to bring peace on earth; I have not come to bring peace, but a sword. For I have come to set a man against his father, and a daughter against her mother, and a daughter-in-law against her mother-in-law; and a man's foes shall be those of his own household"*[54] or *"He who loves father or mother more than Me is not worthy of Me"*[55] or *"Love your enemy."*[56]

The Lord's Prayer has these two faces; it is direct and simple; yet it is profoundly enigmatic at the same time. Popularization is not the act of the Incarnate Word! Religion for the masses has never given good results, for it benumbs and deadens - and not so much the masses as itself.

In the Lord's Prayer, everything is simple yet enigmatic.

Enigmatic: *"Hallowed be thy Name."* How can we ask that? *"Lead us not into temptation"* — yet temptations are necessary for our purification, as the psalmist [57] sang. Every sentence has a polarized meaning.

The Lord's Prayer, the prayer of prayers, is the model for our prayer as Christ wants it to be — it is He who teaches it to us;[58] He wants it polarised: direct and sincere, yet at the same time always transcending our spiritual state of that moment, our capacity and our restricted horizon.

It is good — this is the tradition of the Church — that conscious Christians pronounce it not only out of obedience or a vague feeling, but, as Saint Cyril of Jerusalem says, with intelligence, as far as possible understanding the value of the words taught by Christ.

The Lord's Prayer contains three triads. The first is in the first three verses: *"Our Father who art in heaven"*: Fatherhood. *"Hallowed be thy Name"*: Son and Word; it is in the Name of Christ that the world is saved; He is the Name, the manifestation of the unmanifest Father.

"Thy Kingdom come" or "arrive"; in the ancient Gospel according to Saint Luke it says: *"May thy Holy Spirit arrive."* [59] In Christ's teaching, the Rule of the Spirit and the Kingdom of the Spirit are used interchangeably; so we have here the Holy Spirit.

This is how the first three verses confess the divine Trinity; they form the first triad.

"Thy Will be done on earth as it is in heaven" expresses the one Will, the divine Energy, also the acceptance by the Virgin — the Church — of this divine Will (*"Let it be to me according to thy word"*); this is obedience, the spiritual Church.

"Give us this day our daily [60] bread": this is communion with the precious Body and Blood of Christ, the sacramental Church.

"Forgive us our debts as we forgive our debtors," this is peace, community, brotherhood, the Church, the Ecclesia, union and concord among brothers.

"Thy Will..." introduces us into the mystery of the Church, the temple of the Holy Spirit; *"give us..."* into that of union with Christ; *"Forgive us..."* into the union of members of the Church.

This is the second triad.

The two last verses show the state "outside the Church":

"Lead us not into temptation," [61] into *schism.* We ask that temptations should not separate us from the community. *"But deliver us from the Evil One,"* from *heresy.* Do not let the Evil One take the revealed Truth from us.

A third triad can be distinguished in the Lord's Prayer: *"Our Father... as it is in heaven,"* a confession of our *sonship* of the heavenly Father by grace; *"give us ... our debtors,"* a confession of *Christ Incarnate*, Founder of the Church; *"Lead us not ... from the Evil One,"* a *confession* of the destruction of the kingdom of Satan and of the establishment of the Kingdom of the Holy Spirit. Christ will say: *"The Kingdom of heaven is at hand,"* [62] if the demons are driven away by the *"Finger of God."* [63] The Fathers explain that the "Finger of God" personifies the Holy Spirit, for the Spirit of Life and Truth is opposed to the spirit of death and lying.

So we proclaim the Fatherhood, the foundation of the Church by the incarnate Son, and, finally, victory over the Evil One by the acquisition of the Holy Spirit.

Let us now examine the first triad.

FATHER. We say "Our Father" in Latin, old German and old French.[64] In Greek one says "Father Our." The difference is distinct: "our Father" applies to a natural father; "Father Our" signifies that the heavenly Father, Father of the Son, has become our Father also. We can find ourselves in a spiritual state in which He is not "Father" for us; He is "Father our" when something has changed in us. This is why the Lord said in his Last discourse: *"I have revealed thy Name, Father."*[65]

Nevertheless, "Father" was used in the Old Testament, as well as by the Stoics and Greeks; Zeus is the father of humanity. The notion of divine paternity, a kind of providence bending over his creatures in the manner of an artist looking at and caring for his work, this child which he has begotten, this notion is filled with wisdom and goodness, but it never comes close to the powerful meaning of the divine Fatherhood.

"Our Father"

"Our Father" expresses, first, that the Father of an Only-begotten Son has become our Father; and second, once this has been said, it follows from that that this paternity communicates divine sonship to us. Saint John sums it up ineffably: *"Those who were born, not of blood nor of the will of the flesh nor of the will of man, but of God."*[66]

When we think "Father" in the sense of "our Father," we are not referring to He who suddenly reveals Himself. And for many people, God appears cruel; He seems to abandon his creatures to misery; the absolute Being becomes very uncomfortable. At other times He appears as a Protector whose tenderness bends over His creation, a God unknown and yet attentive: this is a consoling paradox. This second case is a revelation that moves us; we can live from it spiritually, yet it remains incomprehensible.

"Father our" opens the way to quite a different depth, a mark of distinction. God is Father, ours, because we are born of the grace of the Holy Spirit. The Holy Spirit cries in us: *"Abba, Father!"*[67] "Father our" puts us in touch with the spiritual meaning of man, the affirmation that we are not children of the earth, nor of the devil (as Christ names certain people: *"Ye are of your father the devil."*[68] nor of matter, nor of spirit, but that mystically, spiritually, really we are children of God. In a word, "Father our" is the awareness of our divine origin. According to Father Sophrony[69] precisely this consciousness of our divine origin puts everything back in its place, with joy even in penitence and in trials.

A different measure is offered to us: we are not gods by nature; we become gods by grace, through communion and union with it; we bear the divine seed; we are adopted children, but children of God, *"co-heirs with Christ."* [70] And Paul adds: *"Bear God in your body,"* [71] that is to say, recognize that, being his children, you bear Him not only in your spirit but also in your body.

"Our Father"

"Our Father" poses another question: Origen is the first to note it,[72] Saint Maximus the Confessor underlines it. When we say "Father," we imply that there is only one Father: God, and that the other fatherhoods are relative, images, signs, symbols, reflections of the unique Paternity. We are faced with a choice. The Lord's Prayer is a sort of choice, the engagement of a person who realizes what his new vocation is — new although primordial, but forgotten. In saying "our Father," it is *me* who decides; I choose *one* Father who is *my* Father, who is *our* Father (I shall explain later why 'our' and not 'my'), and I no longer recognize any other father than Him. The roots of my existence will no longer sink into nature or other fatherhoods: family, psychical, cultural, spiritual; I have only one Father who is in heaven. I choose, if I may thus express myself, the Tradition whose source is outside time, in God Himself. Our Father comprises the choice.

"He who does not leave his father and his mother is not worthy of Me," [73] the Lord teaches. So should one not honour one's parents? Fatherhoods — cultural, family and others — are worthy of being honoured, like icons reflections of the sole Fatherhood. Let us listen to the others with respect, freely — but the only Father whom we should obey is the heavenly Father. When Mary and Joseph, worried, went back to look for the child Jesus, who had stayed behind in the Temple, He answered: *"Did you not know that I am about my Father's business?"* [74] Let us consider this attitude seriously, for the majority of the world's troubles come from the fact that we look for the source, or fatherhood, outside the one Father. The tragedy begins in the family, grows and is propagated on other levels: national, cultural, spiritual.

Either we are sons of God by grace, or we are not! If we are, we have only one Father. Our father Abraham[75] is only a reflection of the eternal Father. And here we see that 'Our Father' reverses the values completely. The Lord's Prayer is theological. It does not place our existence on something created which rises little by little towards the divine; it turns it around suddenly, placing the head below and the feet above, saying to it: your sun is God the Father. The first of the Hebraic commentaries on the Bible speaks of a tree whose roots plunge upwards and whose leaves and fruits descend downwards (in the sanctuary of our church, you can see on the walls, the same image, a little worn away). The Lord's Prayer is that tree of life with roots planted in heaven. It is a prayer of conversion, of baptism, of penitence or *metanoia* (*metanoia* means reversal).

Without nostalgia, nor desire for God far away, in an instant, it roots man upwards, making him proclaim: *"Father of the heavens, Thou art my only Father; I am Thy son!"*

"Our Father," not "my Father"?

Why do we say "our Father" and not "my Father"?

Christ said: *"I and My Father are one, I in the Father and the Father in Me,"*[76] because He is the *Son* of the Father, while we are the *sons* of the Father.

No one can succeed in realizing and confessing his origin, for we are not isolated individuals; we are Humanity; it is in our reciprocal relationships as brothers in love that the divine is manifested in us. How can we love an invisible God if we do not love our brother? *"Anyone who says that he loves God and does not love his brother is a liar,"* declares Saint John;[77] we are not 'I' when we face God; we are 'we.' Hence the notion of community, communion, unity-collaboration, solidarity among the men who compose humanity, the Church.

Each of us is a son of God as a co-heir, co-son with the others; in each rests the seed of divinity, but this divinity is given to us as a member of the body of Christ.

So our prayer will be: Father! A disinterested recognition[78] of a fact and, at the same time: Our Father, a prayer for myself and for all. The purely personal prayer does not carry; that is why Christ insists: *"Where two or three are gathered together in my Name, I am among them."*[79] This necessarily brings pacification; where peace is absent from the fraternal circle, prayer does not rise up. Sonship is accorded to each in the unity of all.

Let us proceed further and discover the formidable, dialectical meaning underlined by Origen.

God is *our* Father, not your Father. "A formidable word," wrote Origen; so there are some who recognize Him as Father and others who do not recognize Him. Christ will treat the latter as "sons of the devil".[80]

Truly to be a son of God

Man has freedom to recognize God as "our Father" or not to do so. Have you noticed that category of people who appear innocent, sympathetic, humble in appearance, and who will say: *"What do you want; all this is for great people; it is a religion of mystics; we are only little people; we do what we can...?"* This is propaganda of the devil! Before inciting us to pride he incites us to hypocritical humility, stifling in man all consciousness of his origin and of his divine vocation, suggesting to him, under the justification that ambition is pride, that he is no more than dust.

If we truly resolve to be sons of God, our attitude changes and our penitence becomes real. To implore: *"Forgive me, Lord, for I, a son of God, have committed ignoble acts!"* is comprehensible; but if I am only dust, then why should I not steal? To demand penitence of someone who is nothing is nonsense. It is a subtle, very subtle tactic of the demon; he breathes: "You are nothing much; God is far from you; so be simple; be humble." He uses the sacred words of simplicity and humility. The goal of his demagogy is to prevent us from saying "our Father," and so to transform this into the "Father of others."

NOTES

[52]   An allusion to the parable of the prodigal son, one of the most powerful in the Gospel, later commented by the Fathers (Luke 15:11-32.)

[53]   Luke 16: 1-13.

[54]   Matthew 10:34-36.

[55]   Matthew 10: 37.

[56]   Matthew 5: 43-44. Luke 6:27-28.

[57]   Psalm 66:10-12

[58]   See note: P. 31. note 27.

[59]   See. P. 79.

[60]   The French has *substantiel*, while the Greek Bible and some early European bibles had *supersubstantial*.

[61]   The French word here is *epreuve*, which implies trials or tests.

[62]   Matthew.4: 17 and 10: 7. Luke 17: 21..

[63]   Luke 11: 20, Matthew 12: 28.

[64]   And also of course in English. (Ed.)

[65]   John 17:6-26.

[66]   John 1:13.

[67]   Romans 8:15.

[68]   John 8:44.

[69]   Father Sophronious or Sophrony, born in 1896, a disciple of Staretz Silouan on Mount Athos (canonised in 1988), founder of the Monastery of Saint John the Baptist in Maldon (in Essex, in Great Britain) in 1959, where he is the Spiritual Father. Author of spiritual books of the highest order, notably his spiritual autobiography, *His Life is Mine*.

70 Romans 8:17.
71 See 1 Corinthians 6:19.
72 Chap 18.
73 Matthew 10:37.
74 Luke 2: 49.
75 See Matthew 3:9.
76 John 10:30.
77 1 John 4:20.
78 Fr. *constatation*.
79 Matthew 18:20.
80 See John 8:44.

CHAPTER TEN

"WHO ART IN HEAVEN"

The true Creed

From its beginning the Lord's Prayer takes us by the throat, and we can understand that it has always been called the Lord's Prayer, the sacrament of sacraments, or even the true Creed. In fact, the Creed: *"I believe in one God..."* is rather intended for people outside the church,[81] for the catechumens. The Lord's Prayer is the Christian's Creed. When the catachumen is 'enlightened' or 'illumined,' to use the ancient terms, only then is he initiated into the Lord's Prayer. The Roman Church has kept this custom to the present day: in all the public services the Lord's Prayer is spoken in a subdued voice. Until the fifth century, the Christian did not have the right to tell it to the unbaptized; this prayer was not supposed to be known by those who did not yet possess freedom of choice.

Now we sing it aloud, and the reason is simple: formerly the doors of the church were closed from the beginning of the second part of the Liturgy, or the 'Liturgy of the Faithful'; nobody remained but the baptized, and it was during this second part that the Lord's Prayer was sung. Through liberality the Christian Church has gradually permitted everyone to come in at any time. Normally, at the first words of the eucharistic Canon after the common singing of the Creed, the doors were closed and only members of the Church participated in the Liturgy. The deacon cried: *"The doors! The doors! Close the doors! All catechumens depart."* At present we symbolically close the royal doors [82] — but rather as an admonition to late-comers. Ought we not perhaps to reestablish the old custom and really close the doors before the Liturgy of the Faithful and the saying of the Lord's Prayer?

"Who art in heaven"

Although the examination of the expressions "our Father" and "Father our" is far from complete, we shall pass on to the study of the phrase *"Who art in heaven."* Our Lord said many times in the Gospel, especially in that of Saint Matthew: *"your heavenly Father"* or *"my heavenly Father."*

Why is *"in heaven"* linked with the Father? Why does Christ qualify the Divinity, God the Father, as heavenly?

"Heavenly" has several meanings; the direct meaning: Triune God, transcendent, who is not alone but surrounded, as the Prophet Daniel says, by

myriads and myriads of angels.[83] It is impossible to enter into relationship with Him, as His servant or as His son, without taking into account this innumerable spiritual and heavenly host. And here suddenly is the vision of a God who, although transcendent, lives united with His creature, with His cosmos in the absolute sense. The Apostle Paul writes, *"His name is above all names, "*[84] above principalities, powers, all the heavenly hosts.

First meaning: God with the angelic hosts

This brief phrase, *"Our Father who art in heaven, "* reveals to us that outside the lost sheep, humanity, there exist ninety-nine spiritual sheep who have not gone astray:[85] the angelic worlds. The Church teaches that the visible world, or what we call by that name — that is to say the solar system with our earth, and, on this earth, humanity — represents symbolically one percent, and the vast invisible world, the angelic world, represents 99 percent. The world which we see is a tenth (of a tenth of a tenth etc.), one in 9.9999 to infinity, that is, 1 in an unlimited number. The number nine; nine angelic spheres, refers to the infinite. Thus, when we say *"our Father which art in heaven, "* or *"our heavenly Father, "* we speak primarily of our Father who is surrounded by uncountable spiritual worlds.

In the nineteenth century we formed the habit of thinking: God and I. The Lord's Prayer, however, has taught us for many centuries to say: God and we, the Father and humanity; but *"who art in heaven, "* leads us into a world in which he who is our Father is surrounded by higher and incorporeal beings.

One word was enough to place us in what is called angelology. Genesis already refers to the *"Creator of heaven and earth, "* and the Creed confesses the *"Creator of things visible and invisible. "* In the Bible, the term *heaven* designates the spiritual, invisible world, and the term *earth* refers to the material and psycho-material, the visible world. When the deacon Saint Stephen cries: *"Blessed be my God who is the Creator of heaven and earth, "*[86] he is blessing not a God who is somewhere in the clouds, but one Who is the Author of an immense and invisible world. Likewise, in the divine visions — whether that of Moses, that of Daniel, of Ezekiel or of Revelation — *"He who is, "* the unnamable, is surrounded with multitudes of cherubim, seraphim, and the heavenly hosts. This is the direct meaning of *"who art in heaven. "*

Second meaning: the angelic world in man

Let us now approach another meaning: the anthropological meaning. We have all read in Scripture and heard in sermons that our body is the temple of the Holy Spirit.[87] Christ has told us: *"We shall come and dwell in you*; [88] that is to say that the Divine Trinity is not only in the spiritual heights but that it also rests in us. Thus we might say, in a rather simplistic way, that we bear within our human body — and more deeply in our human soul — a spiritual human world with God's dwelling at its centre: three circles. But in the divine dwelling established at the centre of our being, the Trinity is not alone: it is encompassed by its heaven; all the angelic world is in us.

Remember this doctrine: what is higher is interior and what is exterior is inferior. Interiorization raises; exteriorization precipitates down into darkness and the fall. To fall and exteriorise are two notions with identical spiritual value; it is the same with elevation and interiorization.

How can we verify a state of the soul? If your elevation is produced without interiorization, it will be a negative ecstasy, a form of illusion; if your burst upwards is not sustained by a movement towards the interior, you are out of balance. On the other hand, if you enter the depth of yourself without raising yourself towards God, you fall into a different imbalance. These two mysticisms can be controlled. The young are often swept upwards, whence their fall; and the old souls retire within themselves without God, which is why they also fall: all mysticism which summons us to interiorization without elevation will lead us to a purely psychic and exterior world. The criterion of the spiritual life is always twofold: elevation with interiorization.

This having been said, in reality there is in the human being not only the body and the soul, but in him also live the cherubim, the seraphim, the thrones, the throngs of angelic spheres. If God dwells in you, the myriads of angels are as dust beside Him. It is logical. Conceive for a second that you are the temple of the Holy Spirit; understand the depth and complexity of the human being; and you will realize to what extent our consciousness has fallen.

It seems to us — I say 'us,' because it is the general opinion, but I do not know if it applies to every individual in particular — it seems to us that there is something great, illimitable: our body; and then a little point in us, a very little point, comparable to the most minute of those Russian dolls which fit one into another: God. As a child I had an experience of atheist Renaissance style. I knew that there existed in the kitchen garden cauliflowers whose flower is covered with leaves; one day I discovered one ... entrancing. I picked it promptly, pulled the leaves aside to get at the soul in bloom: nothing; I pulled off the leaves ... nothing: emptiness. It was, alas, only an ordinary cabbage. Then I thought: Lord, from now on I shall love atheists, for I have acted like them, I have confused cabbages and cauliflowers. They cut up man's body to find the soul — and they only get emptiness...

The spirit is interior energy, vital force, a geometric point which one cannot define spatially. God and the angels do not occupy space, but let us nevertheless accept a comparison taken from spatial categories. The normal person, not fallen like us, should be considered thus: a vast circle which is God; then our angelic nature, then our psychic nature, and, last, a point balancing in the infinite, similar to a satellite: our body.

The visible cosmic universe is only a piece of dust — if one can speak so — in the limitless ocean of the angelic world, and the latter is only the tip of a point in the divine immensity. Do you grasp the reversal of vision? Since childhood our fragile spirit has been accustomed to look at the world in another way than it is.

And here is another of my experiences ... very curious — one Pentecost, during my sermon on the Holy Spirit which gives life to everything, I suddenly stopped discerning the world — I did not feel it any more... It had become marvelously small, not to speak of myself and the church — the Spirit had taken all the room.

When we sing *"Our Father who art in heaven,"* we mean then that beyond us lives the infinite, angelic, spiritual cosmos, of which we are only a tiny part; that God is not alone, that he is surrounded by saints and angels — and not only that the 'heavens' represent the spiritual heights englobing the universe, but that they are in us.

Third meaning: the Earth raised higher than heaven

But there is a third meaning to this first request of the Lord's Prayer. What is it?

Christ said: *"Our Father who art in heaven,"* and not: *"Our Father who is Father of heaven."*

The Bible calls the angels "sons of God," but the sonship of humanity — and beyond it, that of the visible world — with God, this mystical sonship through the Holy Spirit, of which the Apostle John speaks (*"They are born not of blood nor of the will of the flesh, nor of the will of man, but of God."*),[89] is a special gift attributed to humanity. The angels are far superior to us in a sense, and inferior in another sense. Now the spirit is superior to the earth; heaven to the earth, and we ask that: *"Thy will be done on earth as it is in heaven"*; but because of man, in the ground plan of the divine creation the earth will be superior to heaven. For what is above shall descend and what is below shall rise high; the first will be last, and the last will be first.

It goes without saying that we should do everything to restore to heaven what we have crushed and diminished in ourselves, to place it above the earth. Still this is only a temporary step. For if the hierarchy must be restored, the spirit having submitted to matter or to the psychic and the high invaded by the low — it is in this that the sin of the fall resides — if Our Lord asks that His will realized in heaven be done on earth, even in matter, that what has been accomplished in the angels should be realized in man, in this spirit-matter — God's final thought nevertheless is that matter will be higher than spirit.

How is this possible? The strange rhythm of creation gives us permission to make the statement. The first becomes last, the last first; the small becomes large, the large small, and so on. The *feast of the Ascension* explains it to us: Christ raises human matter above the angelic planes; the Creed makes it clear: *"At the right hand of the Father."* What will be the transfigured flesh, the world transfigured and resurrected? We believe in general that the body contains the soul; in the transfigured world, the soul will bear the body as the angels bear the Virgin Mary in the icons.

We have thus reached another law of the transfigured world: the interior will be exterior and vice versa, the visible world will be invisible and the invisible visible. I cannot here go further into the angelic mysteries.

The third meaning then consists in this, that fatherhood, spiritual fertility are accorded to man. I do not at all mean to say that the angelic cosmos is deprived of evolution, revolution, change in life, but creation belongs to men, and it is in this that human dignity resides. That is why the heavenly Father wants man, through His pre-eternal and only-begotten Son, to become His sons, the sons of the heavenly Father.

Fourth meaning: paternities, icons of the one Paternity

Heaven is full of divinities living through God. Man, matter, and the earth have turned away from Him. This has led to an opposition; heavenly-earthly, spiritual-material, imperishable-perishable, invisible-visible, interior-exterior. Seen from this angle, *"Father who art in heaven"* signifies that this Father is spiritual, heavenly, divine, opposed to the carnal or psychic father and to all the earthly fathers, and that all the true fatherhoods, taking their origin from the heavenly Father, should be transparent, that they should be reflections of the one Father who is in heaven.

NOTES

81 *"Those without"* in the sense used in the Gospel.

82 The doors between the *litei* or nave of an Orthodox church and the *narthex* or "first room."

83 Daniel 7:10.

84 Ephesians 1:21.

85 A reference to the parable of the lost sheep: Matthew 10: 6 and Luke 15: 4-7.

86 A typical example of how this author worked. No matter! Before his martyrdom, Saint Stephen did not say exactly this, but it perfectly represents this attitude. See Acts. 7:59..

87 See for example Saint Paul: Corinthians 6:19.

88 John 14:23.

89 John 1:13.

CHAPTER ELEVEN

"THAT YOUR NAME BE HALLOWED
ON EARTH AS IN HEAVEN"

Having said: *"Our Father Who art in heaven,"* Christ continued: *"hallowed be Thy Name, Thy Rule begin, Thy Will be done,"* then he added: *"on earth as in heaven."*

We will now examine these three phrases, first taking them together, then studying them separately in sequence.

"On earth as in heaven"

Saint Cyril of Jerusalem, Origen, and Saint Cyprien, all state that the phrase *"on earth as it is in heaven"* does not refer only to the will, but also to the two preceding phrases: *"hallowed be thy Name on earth as it is in heaven,"* and *"that thy Rule may come on earth as it is in heaven."* That is to say: Thy Name is already hallowed in heaven, thy Kingdom has already come in heaven, thy will is already realized in heaven, but thy Name has not yet been hallowed on earth, thy Kingdom has not yet come on earth; thy Will has not yet been done on earth.

The Name is already hallowed in the angelic world which remained faithful, the kingdom of God; the Holy Spirit has already come, and God's will is already done, because the angels do his will without a murmer.

Our prayer asks that this will that is already realized, this kingdom that has already come, this Name already hallowed in the angelic world, should be so also in our visible cosmos, and in us. Our prayer entreats that — permit me to use this slightly barbaric expression — these should be *'actualized'* bodily.

That the Name is hallowed, the kingdom come, and the will realised by and for the angels, this we know: the archangels Michael and Gabriel have manifested this. A splendid Byzantine icon represents this: the angels holding up the Logos. But just as the angels exist within us, the Name is already hallowed wherever God dwells; the Kingdom is already come where the Spirit dwells, and the Will is already accomplished within that spiritual plane — that is to say: in us.

On the one hand, we ask in this way that what is realized in the angelic world should be realized on earth, and on the other hand, that what is already realized in the depth of the human being, born of God in the mystery of baptism and of his begetting of Christ, should be manifested outwardly.

We can begin to glimpse the development of this prayer: *"Father"* in heaven; *"Thy Name"*: who is Thy Name? Christ; *"Thy Rule"*: rule and Spirit are one and the same, and the ancient version of Saint Luke said: *"that Your Spirit come"*; [90] *"Thy will"*: what is this will if not the one will of the Three persons? This word contains the whole depth of theology: Father, Son, Spirit — one will; Father, Name, rule — one single will.

Mary's prayer

I shall finish with an anecdote. Praying one evening before the statue of the Virgin which is in our church, I asked her for a long time: what prayer should I repeat? A voice answered: *"The Lord's Prayer."* Often voices from heaven do not seem to us very appropriate ... I thought to myself: short prayers are easier, but I accepted the advice, and in gratitude I murmured: *"Could I not add a prayer for thee, O Virgin Mary, Mother of God?"* And the voice said to me: *"I am in the Lord's prayer."* *"Where?"* I asked. And the virgin continued: *"Thy will be done."*

Yes, these words: *"Thy will be done"* contain the unity of the divine will, and also the whole of mariology; they are the response of the Virgin, and they are the dogma of the Saints and of the Church.

Then, gradually, you will understand that our Creed, our confession of faith, is only a shadow thrown by the Lord's Prayer, the shadow that is revealed to the catechumens. It is for this reason that the early church unveiled the Lord's Prayer only to initiates who had been received into the Church, and never said it aloud in front of those who had not been baptized.

As I said earlier, we ought to read: *"Hallowed be Thy Name on earth as it is in heaven, thy Rule come on earth as it is in heaven, thy Will be done on earth as it is in heaven."* Grammatically, "on earth as it is in heaven" refers to the three phrases, the three steps. I had already told you earlier that the Name designates the world of the Son, the kingdom that of the Spirit, and the will the communion of Saints, the Virgin Mary having responded to the Archangel Gabriel: thy will be done. [91]

Heaven and Hell

"Hallowed be thy Name on earth as it is in heaven": it follows that the Name — the Son — is already sanctified in heaven. I have explained how we should understand the word "heaven." I shall repeat it for emphasis. Heaven is what is above us, the angelic spheres in opposition to the world here below, but at

the same time it is the interior heaven, in the depth of our being, and the opposite of the exterior, the psychic, the corporeal.

Let us not be afraid to say it again, two tendencies govern human religiosity (I say: religiosity); one of these conceives God in spatial terms: God is on high; we are below, and as we pray we lift ourselves up toward Him; the other conceives of religion as within: God is within us, in contrast to what is external. These two tendencies are imperfect, for what is above is within, and what is below is also outside. Hell is the under-sun, the inferior world, the below, the fall and, in Christ's words, *"the outer darkness."* Outer, inferior, *"infernal";* and below all mean the same in our vision of the spiritual world. If, like the mystics, you live solely in the interiorizing conception, or if you do not leave the external vision of the heights, you will fall into incomplete mysticism or an interior piety. The mystic and the pious man are imperfect. The true path does not entail a division. He who prays truly goes inwards, but in going inwards he rises upwards.

The Christian attitude before prayer does indeed consist of placing oneself before God, but also of abandoning the external world and entering into oneself. These two movements coexist, and together they form the Christian act. Let us not allow ourselves to be drawn to superficiality or to a mysticism incapable of understanding the cosmic and universal meaning of our religion. As we free ourselves from the inferior layers of our inner being, we rediscover heaven, and, at the same time, our soul mounts towards the heights.

The names of God

Christ uses two words: *"Hallowed be Thy Name."* Sanctification and Name.

I said to myself, not long ago, that it would be useful to edit a dictionary of Christian words. Through lack of exact understanding a person condemns himself to be unable to plunge with all his being into the teaching of the Lord. The *'verbs'* are precious keys, thanks to which the doors to the mysteries and spiritual realities will open. To define words exactly is to save the world from disorder and to reconstruct it.

Name and sanctification. Have you noticed that the word 'Name' is constantly found in the Scriptures, particularly in the "prayer of priesthood:" [92] *"I have manifested thy Name to men ... I have kept in thy Name those whom thou has given to me ... I have revealed thy Name to them."* [93]

The Name ... to name — an unlimited kingdom! Unnamed things do not exist for Christian thought. Things that are named wrongly are corrupted and things that are truthfully named are transformed. The name pierces the knowledge and the essence of things; it transcends all discursive reasoning, analytical or synthetic; it makes us catch onto something, puts us in contact with that which we name, permitting us by this virtue to change what has been named. A name, consciously and purely articulated, projects such force that the apostle Peter cured a sick person simply using the name of Jesus.[94] This is a fortress and a chariot of war.

The divine name was never written or spoken except once a year, when it was spoken by the High Priest behind the curtain in the Holy of Holies. Until the invention of printing nobody dared to write the divine name in books, but showed it as an abbreviation. There is an analogy between communion — the body and blood we receive — and the name, a vehicle of divinity.

God is seated in His name as every person is seated in his own name. It is for this reason that the great acts of life, baptism or monasticism, are accompanied by a change of name. In Genesis, the Almighty changes the name of Abram to Abraham [95] and that of Jacob to Israel.[96] God manifests Himself by His energies, which pass through us like rays, and by His Names. Read the Old Testament attentively: it reveals these names progressively. We [97] celebrate them before Christmas as the *"Seven Great Antiphons"*; we begin with 'Wisdom' and end with 'Emmanuel', the eighth being 'Jesus';[98] Christ calls Himself the *"Son of man,"* and by giving Himself this name He identifies Himself and becomes humanity.

To name a creature falsely risks destroying it; to name it correctly helps it to become deified, for a name is simultaneously image, definition, and thought. 'Word' will then be, par excellence, the Name of Him who names. And when Christ declares: *"Ask the Father in my name"*[99] he hastens to add: *"and you will receive it."* We tread on the threshold of the unnameable, the indefinable, the indescribeable unknowable mystery: God willingly gives Himself by, names Himself by, a series of names, each of which raises a new horizon; but the name of names is "Logos",[100] and the name of names of the Incarnate One is "Jesus."

The Name of Jesus

This last name possesses the supreme power because in it works the meeting of divinity and humanity: *"You are to give Him the name Jesus."*[101] It is the name of the Word made flesh, of salvation, of realization. The devil fears it. The Christian becomes invincible by it.

On the other hand, with its immaculate transparency, this name illuminates he who pronounces it and He whom it names. The name is the revelation. God names Himself before giving the law to Moses: *"I am He who is;"*[102] *On* [103] is a divine name which God applies to Himself in order to illuminate the laws which Moses is to promulgate. The New Testament reveals the name of the Trinity: Father, Son and Holy Spirit.

On the external plane, the human — let us call it the horizontal plane — we say that the name includes all the teaching of Christ. The Old Testament already says: *"My name has been defiled by the nations,"*[104] *"You will be hated because of my name."*[105] We will be hated by the World because we pronounce the name of the Word, that is, because we speak of his doctrine. When the Prophet cries that the name of God has been defiled by the nations, he accuses them of having distorted God's laws. Here the name is raised like a standard and set out in front like a spokesman.

The power of the name

This reminds me of the Hindu story of the king who, too busy to study, prayed to the wise men of his kingdom to sum up all human knowledge for them. At the end of ten years, ten wise men brought him ten volumes. The king, too busy, said to them "O wise men, paraphrase it." Ten years later they came back with three volumes. The king, too busy, said to them: "O wise men, paraphrase it." Ten more years went by. The three remaining sages returned with a single volume. The king, still too busy, said to them: "O wise men, paraphrase it." Finally, ten more years having flowed out, the last surviving sage approached the king. The great king was dying. The sage then bent over the dying one and said to him in a low voice the name which summed up all the volumes. The great king thanked him and departed with his Name. Here we grasp the close link between unceasing prayer and the Hindu 'mantras.'

And I remember another legend, this one from Brittany. It is the story of a simple, unlettered man who was a devotee of the Virgin. He could only repeat: *Ave.* When he was dead, a plant grew on his grave and remained there, always in bloom. The grave was opened, and it was found that this flower had taken root in his heart.

The power of the name! Consciously or unconsciously, each of us has his word, his prayer, his name.

Hallowed be thy Name

"Hallowed be Thy Name." What is the name that Christ referred to? Grammatically, "Thy Name" refers to the Father, but what Father? That described by the Stoics, bending over humanity like a providence? Christ speaks of the Father of an Only-begotten Son, Father of Divinity, not father of providence.

"Hallowed be Thy Name": this is attached to the Father of the Only-begotten Son, and in reality to the presence of his Eternal Son, to the Word Himself.

"Hallowed"? First let us examine the adjective "holy." *"Holy, holy, holy, Lord God of Sabaoth,"* [106] which we so often use lightly.

"Holy" is one of the names for the manifestation of the transcendent God. God alone is Holy, and if we qualify certain people as 'saints' — the Holy Virgin, Saint John, Saint Dionysius — this is not meant to imply that they possessed heroic virtue, but that they *'collaborated'* with the *Holy*, with *the Holiness* of God. Objects and places can be holy, (the holy cup, [107] the Holy of Holies) through their relation to the One who is holy, sanctified by the intangible presence. Holiness is the resplendent aspect of the majesty of the creator, and sanctification is the blanching of every stain, every shadow, by the mysterious communication of the inaccessible light of the Triune, the unveiling of the glory of the Creator in that which is sanctified.

Grace and sanctity

In order to understand sanctification better, let us put it alongside another term: grace. I have many times spoken of grace and truth in the exegesis of the Prologue of John, [108] trying to define grace as a spiritual joy, an uncreated warmth which invades us deeply and gives us 'wings' of joy. Grace is like the subtle breath, the refreshing rest which fills us with joy.

Holiness, another form of divine manifestation, is different from grace. It can wear the face of a powerful flash of light, and those who see it are seized with holy fear and trembling. *"Take off your shoes,"* God commands Moses. [109] And when the priest declaims in the liturgy *"Holy Things to those that are holy,"* [110] we reply at once: *"One alone is Holy; one alone is Lord, Jesus Christ, to the glory of God the Father,"* for we know that we are not holy, and nevertheless the Church calls the faithful 'saints' — by participation. So it creates in us the double feeling of the myrrh-bearing women [111] on Easter morning, when the Angel asked them: *"Why do you seek Christ among the dead?"* [112] Fear and joy. The Resurrection radiated holiness. They ran to give the news to the apostles with fear and joy. This is the source of our fear and joy at the moment of communion: *"Draw near with fear of God, with faith and love."* [113] The angels, in their transparent holiness and their participation, cry out with fear and trembling: *"Holy! Holy! Holy! Lord God of Sabaoth!"*

The communion of holiness

Sanctification is communication of this holiness. As we sanctify the Gifts, [114] so we sanctify our life.

In imploring God that our life may be sanctified, we form the most audacious request one could imagine. We have the temerity to desire that the

Holiness contemplated with amazement by the angelic Hosts — the purity and splendor of God — should be manifested in our universe, that it should be communicated to us. This is why penitence and purification are necessary, on pain of being burned.

"Hallowed be thy Name on earth as it is in heaven," is asking that the majesty of God be transmitted to transform and transfigure the world, as it transfigured even the clothes of our Lord on Mount Tabor,[115] making them white as snow; we allow ourselves to hope, with Isaiah, that each creature will shine like seven suns.[116] From this point of view we can affirm without error that the second verse of the Lord's Prayer carries the Christian theological notion of the divine beauty which must sanctify everything.

This gospel formulation is the 'pearl of great price' of the missionaries.[117] "May thy gospel, O Lord, be so shining between my hands that the souls will run to thee, captivated by Thy dread beauty." For this holiness should live in us.

The 'mission' often runs aground because we are afraid to ask sincerely: *"Hallowed be thy Name."* We prefer to acquire an imitation, a tranquil little holiness, rather than to receive what God wants to offer, the holiness of the triple unity of the light.

One of the names of this holiness revealed by the Word is that of the Trinity: Father, Son and Holy Spirit.

NOTES

[90] *See Chap 12.*

[91] This is the deep meaning of Mary's response to the angel of the Annunciation: *"Be it unto me according to thy word."* (Luke 1:38.)

[92] "Prayer of priesthood": traditional name for the final prayer which Christ addressed to His Father after the Last Supper and before he was arrested in the Olive garden, during which, as "high priest" par excellence (See Epistle to the Hebrews Chaps 7 and 9) he offers to sacrifice Himself for those whom His Father has given Him. (John 17.)

[93] John 17:6.

[94] Acts 9:40.

[95] Genesis 17:5.

[96] Genesis 32:28.

[97] The Orthodox churches.

[98] Each day of the week before Christmas, the Orthodox Church of France, like today's Roman Catholic Church, celebrates one of the following seven divine Names that follow by a "Great Antiphon". The names are: Wisdom, Adonai, the

Seed of Jesse, Key of David, the Orient, the King of nations, Emmanuel. The eighth name, Jesus, is celebrated on December 24th.

[99] John 14:13.

[100] Or "Word".

[101] Luke 1:31.

[102] Exodus 3:14 - given in the King James version as *I am that I am.*

[103] Greek *Eime ho On,* "I am that I am": a translation in the Greek version known as the Septuagint of the Hebrew *Tetragrammaton* (the Name in four letters) Yod-He-Vau-He, by which God named Himself to Moses and which, to show respect, is never spoken. It is also known as the *Schem ha-Mephorasch,* the unnameable name, the unspeakable..

[104] Ezekiel 43:8.

[105] See John 15:20-21.

[106] This invocation forms part of all Christian liturgies.

[107] That is, the Holy Grail or Sangreal.

[108] We call the first chapter of the gospel of Saint John the "Prologue." It is one of the peaks of the theology of the incarnation of the Word.

[109] Exodus 3:5.

[110] In the liturgies of Saint John Chrysostom and of Saint Germain of Paris.

[111] So-called because they brought myrrh and aromatics to embalm the body of Jesus.

[112] See Luke 24:5.

[113] Spoken by the deacon during the liturgy of Saint Germain of Paris.

[114] The "Holy Gifts": this is the name given, in the Orthodox liturgy, to the bread and wine that have become the body and blood of Christ.

[115] See Matthew 17:1-8, Mark 9:2-8 and Luke 9:28-36.

[116] Isaiah 30:26.

[117] An allusion to the parable of Christ: Matthew 13:45-46.

CHAPTER TWELVE

"THY KINGDOM COME"

"That Your Spirit will come"

"*Thy Kingdom* (or *'rule'*) *come*" is replaced in ancient texts such as the Gospel according to Luke (in the early version in the Codex Sinaiaticus), by "*thy Spirit come*"and not "*thy Kingdom.* "[118] In fact, if we consider the kingdom of God in depth, what is it if it is not the Holy Spirit? I must insist on this thought, because the literature of the twentieth century has abused the word "kingdom." So permit me to open a parenthesis.

The Kingdom

Certain people imagine that the "kingdom" of God is a sort of organization of society in the social and human domain, ruled by a 'Christ-King.' They have made a state of this kingdom. Others see the kingdom more as a family, not in the strict sense of an organisation or of an administration, but of a social arrangement between brothers. Indeed, one can apply this meaning, but it is not the whole truth!

Kingdom or rule, "to seek the Kingdom of heaven and its justice above all, and everything else will be subordinated to it," [119] means something else. The Gospel of Luke explains it: it is the search for the Holy Spirit in life and in ourselves, for, Christ says: "the Kingdom of heaven" is in you and among you; not as an organisation or a social attitude, but as a "*breath of life,*" *in* society and *in* us. To simplify, let us use modern words, theologically inexact but close to our understanding, and say: mentality, environment, climate... Does not one say: "what a good atmosphere!" This "atmosphere" is not something social; it is impalpable, although evoked by light and music, for example. Do we not also say: "the atmosphere of this society is pure, these people have a sympathetic mentality." These images of the psyche make it easier for us to understand what the Lord calls the 'kingdom'; it is the same with the natural meaning — thus the expression 'vegetable kingdom' is closely connected with the environment.

So, when we utter the words: *"Thy Kingdom come,"* let us begin by thinking: thy climate, the divine climate surround us, may the divine atmosphere (the Holy Spirit) penetrate us.

Synergy

On the other hand, let us never forget that prayer without our action, likewise action without prayer, cannot exist. Let us pray in the image of the supplication that will follow: *"Forgive us our debts as we forgive our debtors"*: thy kingdom come as we build it so that it may come; thy name be hallowed in us as we do everything to hallow it, etc ... Prayer is effective if man goes to meet it, then it is one of the forms of *synergy*. He who believes that he can reach perfection by means of methods of meditation without prayer is deluding himself, and he who prays without conforming himself to what the prayer asks is blameworthy: *"Why do you call me: 'Lord, Lord,' and do not do what I say?"* [120]

Towards the kingdom

What is this action which leads to the kingdom?

We can fulfill the commandments of God and still remain outside the Kingdom. We can give our life for our neighbour, die, become poor for him, endure trials and not possess the Kingdom in us at all, nor spread it around us. So what is this action?

We can carry out the commandments because we love; we respect; we obey Christ in a spirit of constraint: I give my last penny to a poor person *because* Christ wants me to. The act is praiseworthy; Christianity is confessed, the name of God hallowed, but by an *effort* made in the name of Christ.

The kingdom will be born when we act this way, but without compulsion, '*naturally.*' Consider a dishonest man who forces himself to be honest because he is converted to Christ; certainly he deserves to be praised, it is right that he begins in this way; he is glorifying God by the fact that, being naturally dishonest, he acts honestly ... But the kingdom is not yet there! It will arise when this man is naturally honest, incapable of being otherwise. If our act transcends our nature, we are still at: *"hallowed be thy name"*; if it is organically bound to us, the kingdom has come.

Let us imagine a nervous, excited, irritable person plunged into a tranquil milieu; little by little, normally, naturally, he will become peaceful and the stage of compulsion will be passed. *"Breathe love,"* said Gregory the Theologian, not only in the name of Christ, but out of a personal need. I do not reject the first state. I only say that it is not yet that of the kingdom.

"Hallowed be thy name" implores the Father for the strength to compel ourselves to do good in the name of Christ, so that this name may be hallowed. *"Thy kingdom come"* in me, on earth, in all, implores of God the grace *to be* prayer and goodness.

Paradoxically speaking: the virtues are as natural to us as our vices. [121] This investigation throws into relief the work or the absence of the Spirit in man.

Is he Christian, a Christian *theophor*, that is capable of heroism, of fervent love for the Christ who died for us, or is he a Christian *pneumatophor*? That is to say, freed of all compulsion, in whom everything becomes supranatural, or rather truly natural, for what we consider 'natural' is contra-natural, and what we define as 'supernatural' is natural. Having passed the first stage, we affirm that what seemed to us to be 'supernatural' is, with the help of God, 'natural': that we have recovered our nature. The prophets express it with a cry: *"I will make of your hearts of stone, hearts of flesh!"* [122]

Work on oneself and prayer

At the beginning of the twentieth century, a certain Mr. Coue started a method of auto-suggestion. He had great success, especially in cases of hysteria; then his method was cast into doubt and discredit was thrown on those who spoke of auto-suggestion. Here I shall put forward a quite simple truth: if auto-suggestion consists in declaring: *"I am not sick, I am not sick"*... when one is sick, in most cases what is the harm in that?

But there exists another method, which seems to be auto-suggestion but is not that at all. We want to pray, we want to be good, and in practice we do not get there; everything prevents us. Is this contradiction normal to man? I do not know — in any case it is a classic state of the soul. You have firmly decided to pray all day, and you find yourself in the cafe engaged in talking with anyone and everyone, provided this avoids prayer; you are invited to dance, and now an easy prayer comes to your lips. Now this method comes in that is analogous to auto-suggestion. It is essentially different in that it contains no contradiction similar, for instance, to that of Coue's method making a sick person affirm that he is not sick. What is its process? How does it remove the external crust which imprisons the prayer?

Let us imagine a man agitated, hungry, nevertheless with interior peace. Should he plunge himself into his soul? The more he plunges into his troubled being, the more the trouble increases, depriving him of the possibility of peace. No, he will first apply himself patiently, very patiently, to not expressing his nervousness. Does he want interior silence? Let him not speak. Is he seething? Let him master this seething by conducting himself externally as he would like to feel internally. Does he aspire to joy when his soul is sad? Let him adopt attitudes of joy; let him say words of joy. This first external effort — the attitude of the theatre — realised, is followed by the battle against thoughts, going from the external towards the internal, the rejection, cost what it may, of thoughts, the stopping of sad thoughts. This is not auto-suggestion; the soul which wants to be joyous or praying simply removes the dust from his way.

I often tell the story of the irritable monk: the Abbot posted him one day at the door of the monastery, ordering him to welcome every inhabitant or visitor of the monastery with this sentence: *"I am happy to see you!"* At first he was seething. It is hypocrisy, you will say? Oh no! The hypocrite is he who conceals his game, without any desire to change his heart, he wants to appear good; whereas this monk acted consciously, wanting to be good. And at the end of several months, our porter was transformed. Such is the virtue of working from the exterior to the interior, work united to prayer.

Perseverance: the three steps

Persist, sustain it, and the prayer will expand the reality of your desire for peace, love and joy. See how excellent this tactic is: the prayer introduces a fifth column, spies, parachutists, who infiltrate into the core of your heart. From inside we blow up the bridges of our adversary and, at the same time, we encircle him with our outward attitudes. To pray is to parachute, to bombard the inner works, to attack the enemy 'from behind.' From the two sides, inner and outer, he is crushed. And suddenly our external gestures, with their theatre and desire, reunite with the patient prayer. They have united together; the compulsion is gone, the kingdom of peace is within our grasp; we live in the kingdom of joy. Even if counterattacks assail us, they will be accidental. The invader is driven out; the Spirit reigns.

Another remark will take us further. It happens frequently that those who wish to do better, to pray more and more easily, do not get there; they feel a violent deception. We see people who are active, energetic in business, steeped in goodwill to enter into the spiritual life, but getting no result. And they cry out: if I do nothing, how can I deserve heaven! I am not going forward, I am not budging! This statement suffers from our lack of will, from the absence of that 'something' which pushes towards the goal; were it only a push, the idea could arise that we have no grace, and this could make us sink into a greyness, a spiritual nonchalance.

The Lord's Prayer warns us: my 'will,' the very fact of being able to pose the question of will, of obedience to the divine will, can only be envisaged after having been through the three stages of the soul:

Our Father who art in heaven
hallowed be thy Name,
thy Kingdom come.

One *can* obey God only after having lived through these three periods. Before this, our attempts fail and will continue to fail; either they will be nourished by ambition or they will not be spiritual and will manifest our extreme weakness: I wish but I am not able!

NOTES

[118] It is the *Codex Bezae Cantabrigiensis* (fifth and sixth centuries) which contains the lesson *eletheo to pneuma sou to agion eph'emas* (that your Holy Spirit come upon us) instead of *elthato he basilea sou* (that your Kingdom Come). But this lesson is very old, as attested by the famous heresiarch Marcion, of the second century, by Tertullian in the third, and by Saint Gregory of Nyssa in the fourth.

[119] See Matthew 6:33 and Luke 12:31.

[120] See Luke 6:46.

[121] This expression of the author is so specific as to be almost obscure. He wished to say that, paradoxically, virtues do not demand an effort of will: that they are as much natural to us — that is to say part of our nature — as are our vices. This links with statements made by Saint Theophan the Recluse that, taken together, appear paradoxical: he once said that Christianity is natural to man, and at another time he said that Christianity demands that we struggle against our nature.

[122] Ezekiel 11:19 and 36:26.

CHAPTER THIRTEEN

"THY WILL BE DONE:"
OBEDIENCE

"Thy will be done," which follows the three first verses of the Lord's Prayer, poses the problem of our obedience to the divine Will.

Psychological meaning of the first three verses

Let us simplify to the extreme — if one can say so — the three first phrases and descend together to the psychological plane, very close to our soul, for if on this plane we discern clearly what they mean, the fact that we were living much more by our 'psyche' than by our spirit confers on us a possibility of realizing the Lord's Prayer in its depth, practically and not only on an intellectual plane.

What then is their psychological meaning?

Our Father is in heaven, He is *heavenly* and we are his children. Psychologically, this is the elevation of the soul. The first attitude will therefore consist in being an idealist, in desiring something great. Children of a heavenly Father, we cannot be worms clinging to the earth. All that lowers and diminishes the human being, all the false humility, will be abolished. I shall call the first impulse a psychological raising of the soul: greatness, idealism, a notion of the divine sonship of man through grace. To see as great: life, and even the enemy! The least 'leveling' is an obstacle to this attitude. How can we fulfill God's Will when we see small? Those who see large are not yet sons of God, but almost.

As soon as the soul is open to greatness, to space, *"Hallowed be thy name"* requires us to accept a style of life appropriate to this elevation. The vulgar, I do not at all say poor, is avoided.

Finally, *"Thy kingdom come"* corresponds to the environment. We may be great and noble in style, but if we still do not create a spiritual climate around us, we are not ready.

Acceptance of the divine will

Let us go a little further. The three first verses reflect the Father, the Son and the Holy Spirit. *"Thy will be done"* dogmatically confesses the creative will of God and at the same time reflects the Virgin Mary — and in her the whole of humanity — arriving, by her acceptance of the divine will, at the second birth. It is, in reality, the response of the world, through the human Mother of God, to the appeal of the Lord and to His Incarnation.

I want to draw your attention to these two meanings of the terms 'earth' and 'heaven': *"Thy will be done on earth as it is in heaven."* We can first understand that the divine Will should be realised on earth, that is to say, in the visible world as it is done in heaven, that is, in the invisible and angelic world. But we can also see it in another way — and some Fathers explain it in this way — that it should be done on earth and in heaven. In this view, it is interesting to note that this accomplishment begins with the external attitude and not the interior. Anyone who thinks that he can begin by interior obedience is mistaken. Obedience in external conduct, acceptance of such and such a test, of such or such a condition, progressively brings interior obedience.

The paradox of obedience

It is evident that this request introduces us to the realm of obedience, the paradox of not begging to receive what we need, for if we pray: *"Thy will be done,"* why pray? That becomes a kind of passive state, leaving it to the divine will. Nevertheless Christ declares: *"Ask and you shall receive... knock and it will be opened to you,"* [123] and if I address myself to God, this is so that my will should be accepted by Him. Does not this verse of the Lord's Prayer contain an apparent contradiction?

Yes, a great effort of will, and a violent battle with oneself, are necessary to yield to Him and to obey Him. Furthermore, the Church teaches us, alongside these words, that we have to almost tear away from God what we desire. On the one hand, our ardent prayer demands; on the other hand, it bows its head: *"Nevertheless, I cannot judge, thy Will and not mine!"* [124] The antinomy arises in our consciousness.

Obedience and inner listening

Obedience is in general poorly understood. Philologically the term obedience in Greek, Latin, and Slavonic signifies: *listening.* Its roots go into 'listening.' Obedience opens the *inner ear*. It is a state which is particularly attentive, not passive. Often, the fraud of the authorities appears here. They mingle obedience to the Spirit with administrative obedience: "You must obey!" This discipline, far from disposing the inner ear, moves the mouth more than in rebellion. All authority which crushes, whatever it may be, the authority of science, of the state, or of the Church, kills the possibility of hearing. People have played on words. Certainly it is normal to obey in the army when it is a question of winning a battle; it is necessary to obey when it is a question of the success of a collective piece of work, but this is in view of a result, of something concrete. The fraud begins the moment religion and the priests use the word obedience in a 'military' way. They destroy the essential, which is to develop the interior ear to be ready always to hear. Obedience frees us, giving us the possibility of being that recipient in whom the Will of God can flow, while external discipline closes the opening.

Thus a monk will obey his Abbot, even if he commands him to go round a table 80 times without reason. First, he gets rid of useless cares: it will be a *positive-negative* obedience; then, he will be freed externally and that will permit him to think of something else. Finally, going round the table — an absurd act — he will rid himself of his prejudices, and, perhaps, of his 'opinions', opening himself to listen, because... not having ever before gone round a table, the position set him seems an absolute 'dogma,' and here the dogma is broken in his soul, preparing him to be available.

But when the religious hierarchy commands us: *"Do not concern yourself about it; obey; dogmas are the concern of theologians; do this and you will be saved,"* then what are they freeing us from? The cares of the world? Not at all! They are freeing us — if one may say so — from God, even from spiritual experience, precisely from what they should bring us to.

It may be that a doctor who is taking care of our body does not describe our illness to us, for the important thing is our healing; but obedience, on the contrary, is the escape from all that could prevent us from hearing. How often this word is dishonestly exploited! Whatever your preferences, when Karl Marx proclaims that religion is the "opium of the people," his words contain a measure of truth. Under the pretext of revelation, under the pretext that the truth has come from on high, we are commanded to obey parents, priests, the State, this person and that; and to await the reward after death. Here, I should affirm, the greatest crime is perhaps to have distorted a number of Christian words; we begin by applying to them a little inexact shading, and suddenly, one day, we perceive that their meaning has changed entirely.

Obedience and liberty

Christian obedience is not disinterestedness; we free ourselves from all we can possibly be freed from so *that we* can *'listen'* better and better to the Word.

Why is the Church in the West so occupied with social work just now? Is it afraid that we were beginning to think, beginning to see ourselves falling into heresy? Ah! If the admirable Roman organization suppressed material worries — taxes, for instance — I would be the first to say to them: "Bless you!" For now we could truly obey, and return to the monastic plane again, whose goal is to give man back freedom of spirit and soul.

Personally I have never tasted freedom as well as behind the barbed wire of my captivity in Germany. Like an Archangel Michael, Hitler had organized those little paradises. We were housed and fed; badly housed and badly fed, but all expenses paid, with a great expanse of sky over our heads. And to preserve us from the wicked world, he had stretched barbed wire and posted his angels: the sentries. It was remarkable...

Alas! *obedience*, admirable in its religious meaning, this word has become irreligious, a spiritual deception. It is urgent to restore to it its original powerful and Christian meaning.

NOTES

[123] Luke ll: 9 and Matthew 7:7.

[124] This was the attitude of Jesus at Gethsemane: Matthew 26:39, Mark 14:36 and Luke 22:42.

CHAPTER FOURTEEN

"THY WILL BE DONE": SYNERGY

Let us try to explain the apparent paradox which we touched on in the last chapter: the union of our resignation to the divine will, on the one hand, with the persistence of our requests taught by Christ on the other. We implore; we insist: *"Knock and it will be opened to you"*; we pray for the sick, to stop trials, to obtain joys; and, on the other hand, we say with a certain fatalism: *"Thy will be done."*

Choosing the divine will

Are we in fact faced with a contradiction? There are three phases: thy will, my will, and *"thy will be done."* God is so powerful that I can do nothing when faced by Him. His will transcends all my possibilities. But then my will enters into play, (my desire that the divine will be done), for it will not be done *if I do not ask Him.* It is not just abandonment to divine will; it is our will which comes to wish it and beg for it.

What do these words mean: *"Thy will be done,"* if not the existential knowledge [125] in our soul, in our whole being, that God is more intelligent, better than we! You will reply to me: this is obvious. No, it is not as obvious as you think. This evidence is revealed in the intellect, but in the human psyche it is not at-all obvious. Let us make a curious, honest experiment: let us rely on God's will, as soon as fear arises, beyond our strength, and if the hand of the Lord will be heavy, if he demands of us something beyond our capabilities, and if, and if... We are afraid that He does not take into account our little desires, our little will, our little impossibilities. To recognize His all-powerfulness and our incapacity, it seems to us, is fatalism, the result of a broken heart.

"Thy will be done" is precisely the opposite of resignation, it includes the movement of an active human will which *wishes* and *chooses* God's will as best for itself.

Voluntary acceptance, the opposite of resignation

Let us try to get to the bottom of this so-called contradiction, for the process of the human soul presents an immense difficulty. How many times in my life I have avoided saying wholeheartedly: *"Thy will be done,"* in apprehension of hearing God ordering me to do something painful, to make a disagreeable effort of psyche. Did He not call Abraham to sacrifice his only son? [126]

And here we are: the moment when we accept voluntarily, not through passivity in the face of His power, but through confidence in His goodness, at the moment when we are ready to give our son, that is to say, what is dearest to us, when we are disposed to respond to the Lord: everything which happens to me, I take it without sacrifice, I abandon myself to Thee, for I am not a servant submitted to a capricious master; my will meets Thy will; at that moment, at the last minute, appears the hand which stops the knife. And we receive a gift superior to all that we could have hoped.

Let us know how then to distinguish resignation from the recognition by our 'psyche' of the very good will of "our Father who art in heaven". Let us insist: man can cry: *"God is good!"* As soon as man enters into conscious contact with Him, doubts rise, the divine greatness takes on a transcendent and dread face as it views our weakness.

I would say that the attitude of *"Thy will be done"* is not even that of a son towards his father (frequently the human father is a master for his child), but that of a small child before his mother, or still more: towards a grandmother who pampers and forgives. The 'pampering' of our God is at the end of the narrow passage, and a superabundance of grace followed Isaac's sacrifice. Have no reservations toward Him, and He will have none toward us.

My will and 'Thy will': One will as one

Finally, my will and 'thy will' are only one will, a synergy, one will as one.

What does one generally ask of God? A thousand things, money, love, prayer, power, intelligence. We begin by demanding: *"give, give,"* then approaching Him we come to murmer: *"nevertheless, thy will!"* And an unexpected phenomenon takes place. The soul, sensing that it realizes the divine will, prays more and more ardently, the two wills become communicating receptacles, the ineffable mixture is established because we will it. This stream of water, this circulation of flame become ours progressively, and ours becomes that of God. We express this, for example, in the Eucharist: *"Thine own of Thine own we offer Thee; in all and for all."* [127] We offer God what is God's, God Himself, but it is we who offer Him!

The meaning of unanswered prayer

When prayer is unanswered, what does this mean?

It is admirable! It is always the beginning of something greater. A prayer answered by divine condescension, although outside the divine plane, is not always the best solution and can produce unsuspected difficulties. I have known people who, praying unceasingly for years, finally obtained the object of their desires; they sometimes paid a heavy price for it... On the contrary, unanswered prayer is, in principle, a step towards a blossoming out. At one time in my life I almost lost my sight; for three or four days I was in a state of blindness. A friend advised me to have myself healed through anointment with the holy oil of the Archangel Michael. I did not do it, because I felt clearly that this trial of losing my sight could give me something new, a distance between the world and my thought, a separation from a multitude of useless things, an increase of inner attention, a fresh and perpetual vision of the invisible, etc... It is necessary to understand — every request not answered: for money, health, affection — conceals a superior wealth that is within our reach.

Recapitulation of the Lord's Prayer

Let us recapitulate the Lord's Prayer in another way. *"Our Father who art in heaven:"* we enter into the reality; we exist, not for ourselves, but as children of the Father; *"Hallowed be thy name:"* we are known by God; *"Thy rule come:"* loved by God, we are alive; *"Thy will be done:"* we are wanted by God, desired by Him... to be desired by God! *"Thy will be done on earth as it is in heaven:"* here we are the object of the divine will and desire.

And also:

"Our Father who art in heaven:" our heavenly sonship, the pledge of our immortality. We cannot disappear: but, being sons of the Father, calling Him "Father," Him, the eternal living One; rooted in Him, we are eternally, not through immortality of the soul, but through Himself. *"Hallowed be Thy name"*; our immortality is conscious, we have consciousness of it. *"Thy rule come:"* the rule of the Holy Spirit; our conscious immortality will be more and more alive. *"Thy will be done on earth as it is in heaven:"* our conscious, living immortality will be creative; for if rebellion and disobedience lead to sterility in man, acceptance and desire for the will of God open anew the domain of creation. This justifies the thought of Archimandrite Sophrony [128] that we shall create in the ages to come, God being in us. These words do not indicate a road from below upwards, but the mysterious *afterlife*, a post-transfiguration road of the world.

Let us finish this picture of the Lord's Prayer.

"Give us this day our supersubstantial bread:" our conscious immortality, living, creative blossoms in the supersubstantial Bread: the communion. *"Forgive us our debts as we forgive our debtors:"* our conscious immortality,

living, creative, blossoming, will be in common, in participation with our debtors. *"Lead us not into temptation:"* our conscious immortality, living, creative, blossoming, common, fraternal, will not show any fissures of hesitation. *"But deliver us from the Evil One:"* no further possibility of a fall.

NOTES

[125] Here the word in the French is *reconnaissance* - recognition.
[126] See Genesis 22:1-18.
[127] Liturgy of Saint John Chrysostom.
[128] See P. 63 note 69.

CHAPTER FIFTEEN

"GIVE US THIS DAY OUR DAILY BREAD"

We reach the heart of the Lord's Prayer, the fifth request: *"Give us this day our daily (or supersubstantial bread.)"*

As children of God we identify ourselves with the Son through the sanctification of the divine name within us. We become a temple of the Spirit, calling for the coming of the kingdom. We realize synergy through our voluntary entry into the world of the deification of our being. One could think that this says everything! But no, we have reached the domain of the sacrament: of God as food.

The mystery of food

Food is granted to man to nourish his life. It is certain that the organism which does not eat dies. Nevertheless, food has become a safeguard only since the original sin. Its role in the "world before sin," or in the transfigured world, is one of development, not of conservation. To feed oneself and so develop oneself and so blossom out into eternity — *"He who eats my flesh and drinks my blood has eternal life, and I will raise him up on the last day."* [129] This is a communion with lasting progress, an enrichment without end of all that is in us.

God does not feed himself; He nourishes his creature. To understand the meaning of all the mysteries (I use the word 'mystery' in the Greek sense, that is: sacrament) is always to rediscover the mystery of food.

The food mystery, the communion mystery, is revealed in two forms.

I repeat, God cannot feed Himself, since He is the Source: the Being; on the contrary, the creation, itself non-being, can be only through communion in God. From the African to the Hindu, all the ancient mysteries are basically a banquet.

The devil's food

There exists a second manifestation of the mystery, very widespread, in which man tries to nourish the divinity, whether by an offering of rice, honey, flour, milk, whether by immolation of animals, bulls, oxen, he-goats or even virgins. This so-called food presented to the divinity is, in reality, feeding the devil. Realize this, that in their underlying meaning these sacrifices to divinities are not offerings to the Almighty, who has no need of them, but to him who is always hungry.

Why the devil? Because the devil is a pure spirit whose power over the world lacks one thing; and haven't you noticed that what we do not possess seems in general the most precious? This feeling is pushed to the extreme in the father of lies; he is tortured by a constant jealousy: he can be neither man nor matter.

This rage is so acute that on the one hand he tries to convince us by every means that matter is detestable and, on the other hand, he is pleased to devour with a gaze the carnal delicacies which it is impossible for him to consume. His hatred of the Incarnation is such that he struggles to prove that Christ is not really man. His thirst for blood, which he does not possess, runs throughout the history of humanity; he is hungry, for having refused the divine grace, the food of the angels, he is greedy, above all, for the world. And in the world, he is greedy above all for the tenth angel which is humanity, that strange being, neither flesh nor spirit, a small part beast, a small part vegetable, a small part angel, a small part God, not knowing very well himself who he is. Furthermore, Christ came for such a being: a completely unbearable thought for the demon, hence his pathologically vital need to obtain blood sacrifices. He is nourished only spiritually, without doubt, since, lacking flesh, he will not know how to eat, but he feeds on both psychic and spiritual substance.

This state is comparable to the enjoyment of the sight of sin committed by another; *sin-watching* is much more serious than an evil action. From this angle, imagination wrongly oriented is more destructive than the act of sin. The Satanic eucharist is the foundation of the devil's food and forms the basis of all the religions desirous of appeasing, of 'buttering up' the principle of iniquity who reigns over men.

God, taking into account human infirmity, progressively substituted himself for the adversary. When, in the Old Testament, He accepts bulls, he-goats and oxen on His altar, it means: "Otherwise, O men, you would bring them to the devil; so at least offer them to my wrath." And men, having begun to sacrifice to the True God, became accustomed to turning their hearts towards Him. After this, God sends out His prophets, crying: *"I abominate your bloody sacrifices!"* [130]

Finally, Christ abolishes them, becomes incarnate, and replaces the food brought by man to the divinity, by the divine food given to man by God.

I have gone on to this brief statement, which deserves to be studied in greater depth, to introduce you to the sacraments and to the sacrament par excellence: the Eucharist.

The Word teaches us: *"Give us this day our daily (or supersubstantial) bread."*

Bread, at least for the West, is the essential food. The East would say: "rice." To ask for bread is not a luxury, but a necessity without which we could not live. In recent times people have taken these words in the literal sense. This is not a mistake: give us what maintains life, so that material problems will not disturb us beyond measure; in other words; free us from the useless cares of this world. We should take this attitude into consideration. We frequently hear it said that it is easier to live in a monastery than in the world: no more taxes, no children, no fear for the future, etc., etc. I will reply, without dwelling on the spiritual difficulties which monks encounter, that one of the goals of the monastic life is precisely to be freed from cares, for difficult sacrifices have no 'a priori' value. A man who makes his life especially painful is impossible for himself and others to live with. Social reforms, Christian socialisms, consist not in procuring justice or comfort above all, but in making life easier; all else is false romanticism. That a shock can release the flavour of the spiritual life is, I agree, beneficial, but the Christian life cannot depend on daily electroshocks. That it is indispensable to overcome obstacles is true, but we should always applaud and collaborate as far as possible in the efforts which make life easier. The modern danger resides in the fact of creating and adding useless needs, confusing that which lightens the burden of existence with that which excites it. Thus, selling on credit is questionable, for example, as while it makes things easier, it often engenders new demands.

The divine thought is: Lord, *"give us today the essential."* This fifth request is indispensable. It envelops also another reality: the Church sees in it communion with God. This communion is manifested doubly: Christ answers the devil: *"Man does not live by bread alone, but by every word which comes from the mouth of God."* [132] Communion is then expressed both by the Word and by the Eucharist.

The food of the word

The West has undergone a curious phenomenon: the Protestants in practice do not want to feed on anything but the Word, while the Roman Catholics do not take sufficient account of it. Although they preach and read the Gospel, they remain centred on the Host, forgetting that the teaching is double: word and communion.

When I say that Protestants feed only on the Word, this is only half true. I remember a conference which I held before a number of pastors at the protestant Institute of Theology at Montpellier. The subject was the place of Holy Scripture in the Orthodox Church. When the conference was over, several listeners said to me: we thought that you would speak of icons, of the Fathers of the Church, of the liturgy, of Dostoyevsky, and you dealt with our subject, the Holy Scripture in itself. Yet we had the impression that you were speaking of a Holy Scripture which we did not know! Since then I have realised the cause of this reaction. I said, for example, that it was necessary to read the Psalms without wanting to comment on them at once; reading them will first *leave its mark* in us and work to transform the interior. Now Scripture is, for most people, a text which is commented on as soon as it is read. This allows one to adopt an attitude immediately. The words, the Word, have not had enough time to go deep into the heart, to be eaten, to be drunk; they are not assimilated. Holy Scripture is no longer a spiritual food, but more of a directive, a master teaching from outside.

No! My friends, we do not have to grasp it at once; we should receive the Word as we take in food. It will work in us and clarify our intelligence. Let us listen to the reading of the Gospel 90% and reflect 10%. And our reflection should not depend on our comprehension in that moment. We are on the threshold of a mysterious kingdom: the food dispensed by Holy Scripture. Here is the meaning of the canonical books: if you read them as books of external law, you run the risk of making all sorts of heresies spring up, for inevitably you will underline what pleases or impresses you. Your soul will register or reject this or that psychological aspect. The food of Holy Scripture should imperceptibly inform the intelligence and release the antennae which will pick up the 'true gnosis.' It is this motif which made the Fathers of the Church avoid calling the Scriptures 'authorities.' The Canon[133] is first a nutritious inspirer, then a master, then, if one can say so, a 'supervisor.'

The eucharistic food

The eucharistic food is veiled in symbol, and we commune then with God, and with the world transfigured as it is. Experience proves it: the more a person communes, the more he is organically strengthened in the spiritual life. The best attitude with respect to communion is to consider it as daily bread, but divine: a simple daily necessity. Its effects are not immediate. I would rather say that it is like homeopathy, or a medicine like penicillin. The consequences of communion are observed in the course of an entire life, in groups, and it is interesting to see how much the spiritual sense diminishes in periods of the history of the Church when communion is almost non-existent. This phenomenon is concrete to the point where it materializes in statistical data.

As to the term *"this day,"* the Fathers agree in saying that is refers to daily communion. Communion with God should never be a project, but an act of "this day."

NOTES

[129] John 6:54.

[130] Isaiah 1:11 and following. (In one translation one phrase says: *'Stop bringing meaningless offerings.)'*

[132] Matthew 4:4.

[133] 'Canon' is a Greek term that signifies 'rule' and defines the rules put into operation by the Church for its own use. The 'canonical' books are those which the Church has selected as essential as a vehicle for the Revelation; they are inspired by the Holy Spirit.

CHAPTER SIXTEEN

THE LAST THREE REQUESTS
"FORGIVE US OUR DEBTS AS WE
FORGIVE OUR DEBTORS"

With mercy and humility

If I am strong and fair, God will be strong and fair with me... I fear this category of virtues because of my weakness; they give me a power, but they are opposite to the divine Virtues! Christ said: *"Judge not that you shall not be judged."*[134] *"Forgive us our debts as we also have forgiven our debtors";*[135] I prefer to treat people with mercy and humility so that they treat me in the same way.

A man deceived me for two years. Until now I have wanted to ignore it and act as if he had not abused me, in the hope of seeing our Lord adopt similar conduct towards me. For if the laws disappear some day, one alone will remain: as you have forgiven, God will forgive you.[136] Here is the kernel of the angelic revelation, immense, dread, imposing; this revelation is linked, tied to the relationships with 'others'; it is social. Do not forget that when we are told to be good to our brothers, it is not at all because they need it, but to call forth God's goodness upon us; God, being identified with each person, is our neighbour. I will then leave the great and virtuous people to judge their neighbour since they will be capable of enduring the judgement of God. Myself, I cannot. Excuse me, I will have pity on myself; I will be weak. Do not imagine that it would be impossible for me to know, for example, the instinct of an Ivan the Terrible. (Perhaps I could kill.) During a shipwreck one simply holds onto a plank, bent on not sinking; me, I clutch hold of one single certainty: to have extreme indulgence towards my brother in order to find this indulgence between the hands of our Father. You will respond: *"You run the risk of losing souls!"* I will answer you that I am not strong enough, not great enough to save souls. Now it is enough for me not to lose my own completely, the one which God has entrusted to me! Our soul is not our property; it is a precious vessel which must be transported.

This is a confession, but beyond my personal attitude, which is not indispensable, one can be great and not forgive: the majority of people consider that they have the right not to forgive debts... I doubt this.

Forgiveness of debts: the foundation of the church

This supplication: *"Forgive us our debts,"* is the basis of the Church as a society, which is the reason for all the injunctions of the Gospel; it also indicates the Second Coming[137] which is now being realized.

We could never judge our neighbour if the Second Coming of Christ were present to our spirit, for who will be the judges of this ultimate tribunal? Our conscience, that is to say our conduct towards our brothers, and God with respect to our conduct towards them. Besides, all will be visible, our sins as well as our virtues. So it is not necessary to be ashamed of discovered sins, only to do penance. Besides, the Last Judgement is not the end of time, it occurs in the present, conditioned by ourselves.

Our steps weave theologies. Are we fair? We trace the theology of a just God. Are we people of sacrifice, a little tragic? Our God takes on the look of sacrifice. Are we indifferent? God will be indifferent.

When this legend spreads that in our parish of Saint Irenaeus we 'feel' community, and that it is less so in others, I would cry: *My friends! Community or not, I do not know, but there is one real thing: true community grows where every member progresses in forgiveness, and every time we progress in not reclaiming debts, we are increasing the Church, we are building it.* To build without forgiving debts is to summon the judgement of God.

"And lead us not into temptation": Trials are not possible unless God allows them

Let us first put a principle: evils and temptations cannot arise if God does not permit it. We read in 2 Kings that the Lord will deliver Jerusalem to Nebuchadnezzar,[138] in chapter 42 of Isaiah, verse 24: *"Who has delivered Jacob to pillage, and Israel to the spoilers? Is it not the Lord? We have sinned against Him."*[139] We all know, in the Book of Job, the passage in which Satan comes near the Throne of the Lord and asks Him to deliver Job to him, and God replies: *"Here is everything which belongs to him, I deliver it to you; only do not lay your hand on him."*[140]

When Jesus is summoned before Pilate, does He not declare to him: *"You would have no power over Me if it had not been given from on high?"*[141] Thus temptations require divine permission.

Then why this phrase in the Lord's Prayer? Do not trials really purify us? And he who has not known temptation, says Ecclesiastes, has not passed his trials.[142] Theoretically speaking we can, of course, grow without suffering, but in practice we find that it is when we go through the wine-press that we are strengthened. By failing a hundred times with a picture, we make a masterpiece. And Saint James in his first General Epistle develops it: *"My brothers, regard as a subject of complete joy the different trials to which you can be exposed."*[143] Finally, in the Psalms, God *"tries the minds and hearts"*[144] and plunges us into the crucible, into the fire, and into the water in order to take us out again and give us happiness.[145] What saint, what man of the Church is seen to go through life without trials?

"Lead us not into temptation." Certain people practice a false doctrine: *hoping* for trials; we should not look for them. Saint Cyril of Jerusalem gives us an explanation of this seventh phrase of the Lord's Prayer: "tempt," in Greek, and still more in Hebrew, almost corresponds to *'submerge.'* Lord, make it that we should not be submerged by temptation. We ask to be good swimmers, says the same Cyril, knowing how to swim through the waves to arrive at the port. Do not let us founder; do not let us sink! This request has no other meaning.

Call on divine assistance

Nevertheless here we come to another question: if God permits temptations, he never tempts us beyond our strength, say the Scriptures.[146] So why ask not to succumb?

Surely this is an external and superficial logic! We can only be good swimmers on the express condition that we ask for divine help. It is the same in the liturgy: the Word wants the consecration of the bread and wine; nevertheless all we do is obey his order: *"Do this in remembrance of me,"* then we ask: *"Send thy Spirit."*

Yes, God gives us trials because He knows that we can swim, and yet we should ask Him to help us: God, not as goal, God, not as cause; God always as our help, our collaborator!

Christ emphasises: *"Watch and pray lest you enter into temptation."*[147] The Apostle Peter, who walked on the waters — the waters are the temptations — began to sink, and if Christ had not reached out his hand to him, he would definitely have sunk.[148] Peter was animated by a great desire to go towards God; Peter was moved by a great faith, he lacked prayer. At that moment he lacked that state of prayer in which we need divine help for the least thing, that help which makes our soul walk on the waters of grace.

The formulation of Calvin and of Ignatius of Loyola: "To the greater glory of God," is inexact, in the sense that the motive of the glory of God is insufficient; it has no need for us. God loves us to work with Him, in Him. I will even say that He appreciates a piece of work whose aim is not always exceptional, if it is executed with prayer: help me; lead me not into temptation, I am weak. I would propose to you an image: God places His immaculate lips on the lips of our soul. That is why we must always pray, and when we discern His Will, there is nothing else to do but bend to it: we will have the strength necessary to realize it.

The Love of God, and Perfection

It is evident that in praying to God to free us from temptations, we are asking Him to free us from all that could separate us from Him. Invisibly Christ puts two weights in balance: love of God, and our own perfection. For perfection it is better for us to go through the crucible and conquer ourself; to love God, it is better not to be perfect. How much better it is to be with Him than to compose one's perfection. I have seen souls slow their spiritual ascent because they wanted to be perfect. The construction of the marvellous temple around them prevented the Word from getting in. I will go further: to become a saint, give up the taste for holiness.

"And deliver us from the Evil One:"
Evil does not exist

Evil does not exist. What exists is not evil; it is different aspects of being. Evil is a personal state of consciousness. The Evil One is; the bad deeds are; evil in itself is not.

The evil one falsely combines truths

When the evil one acts, he makes use of a multitude of falsely assembled truths. In Genesis the devil speaks the truth malignantly: "*You will be like God.*"[149]   It is true. You will have knowledge, it is true, he did not lie. He emphasised these truths in order to turn Adam and Eve away from God and make them lose his friendship. Does the evil one slip us into traps by lies? No, by truths arranged in such a way that they become deadly; this is why he is called the evil one. False things break down of themselves. Thus, he wants to convince us, as he tried to convince the Living God, through the words of Scripture;[150] the way he puts them together is such that they detach us from our divine sonship. He tries to make us his children. Christ, in a moment of anger, thunders: *"You are not children of Abraham but of Satan."*[151] To reach his goals he cooks up all the truths; through a little crack he introduces a virulent virus; insensibly he turns us away from the "Father who is in heaven." He communicates to us the impression that we are divinities; he does this by means of despair or pride, it does not matter which!

"Deliver us from the Evil One" comes in when we are already on a level with the luminous perspective of the children of God. Never forget that our life has fissures in it. We are full of interior joy, free from all fetters, vibrant with grace, at the door of life eternal, united to God; even then let us never forget, at the door of life eternal, until the end of time, there is a possible crack through which the Evil One's seduction can slip in.

NOTES

[134] Matthew 7:1.

[135] Matthew 6:12.

[136] See Luke 6:37-38.

[137] Of Christ at the last judgement: Matthew 25: 31-45.

[138] 2 Kings 24:1-4.

[139] Isaiah 42:24.

[140] Job 1:12.

[141] John 19:11.

[142] Reference to Ecclesiastes 34:10 untraceable

[143] James 1:2.

[144] Psalm 7:9.

[145] Psalm 66:10-12.

[146] See Saint Paul, I Corinthians 10:13.

[147] Matthew 26:41.

[148] See Matthew 14:28-31.

[149] Genesis 3:5.

[150] An allusion to the temptation of Christ in the desert: Matthew 4:1-11 and Luke 4:1-13.

[151] See John 8:39-44.

CHAPTER SEVENTEEN

CONCLUSION TO PART TWO

What is remarkable in the Lord's Prayer is that Our Lord does not teach us to begin with *"Deliver us from the Evil One"; "Forgive us our sins,"* but with the more positive: *"Our Father,"* that is, with a total confession of our divine sonship; then, as soon as we have sanctified the name of the Word, and have lived this sanctification which transforms us; after we have implored the Spirit to fill the smallest atom of our being, and accepted with the Virgin all the Will of God; then we ask for the Eucharist, the daily Bread; our attitude towards the neighbour only comes after that. How much easier it is to forgive debts when one has fully lived what goes before. It is only at the last, steeped, armed, and protected, that we add: *"But deliver us from the Evil One."*

In pronouncing the Lord's Prayer, persist one thousand times with *"Our Father who art in heaven, hallowed be thy Name, thy Kingdom come"*; 700 times with *"thy Will be done"*; 500 times with *"Forgive us our debts as we forgive our debtors"*; fifty times with *"Lead us not into temptation,"* and ten times with *"But deliver us from the Evil One."*

The supplications of this prayer should not be lived equally: let the first verse flood you, inundate you! For the Lord's Prayer is constructed from the top downwards.

And to end, if *"Forgive us our debts as we forgive our debtors"* makes us already live the last judgement; if in the eschatological sense: *"Lead us not into temptations"* signifies: *"when the trial of fire comes, make it so that I will not be consumed"* — for God will test us by the fire of His Love. Make it so that the flame of Thy Mercy does not burn me, but warms me! For, behind the sufferings — so sublime is the mystery — is the trial of the fire of the Love of the Trinity for us. If *"But deliver us from the evil one"* makes us accept without reservation that we shall be deified by God, invaded by Him, filled with Him, shall be nothing outside of Him, this is to save us from the last malice of the demon: the last danger of being devoured, of being crushed by the divine Power and the divine Love. To understand His words, it is necessary to disappear, to desire nothing other than "God *all* in all." This is what is called the 'second death.' Then the transfigured world will burst and God will say to us: *"You are not only Me; you are My friends."*

And having prayed in this manner, let us say

Amen! Amen! Amen!

PART THREE

SOME COMMENTARIES BY THE FATHERS ON THE LORD'S PRAYER

CHAPTER EIGHTEEN

COMMENTARIES BY ORIGEN

After the brief commentary above, we shall now offer a few passages from the writings of the Church Fathers about the Lord's Prayer. We will first quote Origen (third century), then Saint Cyprien of Carthage (third century), and finally, Saint Cyril of Jerusalem (fourth century,) author of the famous *"Mystagogical catechism"*.

Origen writes: [152]

"Our Father who art in heaven"

"We must investigate carefully whether there is a single prayer in the Old Testament which calls God 'Father'. Until now, despite our efforts, we have not found one. We do not mean that God is not called Father, nor that true believers are not called the children of God, but nowhere, in a single prayer, is God named Father as did the Saviour in his most intimate address which He has transmitted to us.

"We often find that God is called Father and those who have responded to the call of God are called sons, for example in Deuteronomy: '*You have abandoned the God who begot you, you have forgotten the Lord who created you.*'[153] And again: '*Is it not Him who is your Father, who has held you as his own heritage, who has made and created you*'[154] And further on he says: '*My sons have lost faith.*'[155] In Isaiah we find: '*I have engendered children, I have raised sons and they have abandoned me.*'[156] And in Malachi: '*The son honours his father and the servant reveres his master, If I am thus your father, where in you is the fear and respect that I am entitled to?*'[157]

"Therefore, if we call God Father, and call those His sons who are born of Him because they came to hear his word, even then we will not be able to find anywhere in the ancients any exact and clear affirmation of this sonship. The passages we quoted show that those described as sons should be better regarded as subjects. We can see this from the Apostle's statement that: '*As long as the heir is underage, although he is autonomous in everything, he is in no way different from the slave; he is put under the authority of tutors and guardians until the date determined by his father.*'[158]

The Spirit of Adoption

"The fullness of time is with us with the Incarnation of our Lord Jesus Christ when those of goodwill become adopted according to the teaching of Saint Paul: '*Let it be known that you have not received the spirit of servitude to relapse into fear: you have received the spirit of adoption which enables us to cry: Abba, Father!*'[159] And from the Gospel of St. John: '*But to all who have received Him, who believed in his name, he gave power to become sons of God.*'[160]

"Because of this spirit of adoption, the Roman Catholic epistle of Saint John says of the children of God that: '*Whoever is born of God does not sin, because he bears the divine spark within him, He cannot sin, because he is born of God.*'[161]

Let us behave as true sons

"Now if we reflect seriously on the meaning of these words of Saint Luke: '*When you pray, say Father,*'[162] let us be very careful about calling Him by this name if we are not true sons. Otherwise we surely run the risk of adding to all our sins that of impiety. Let me express my thought more clearly: in his first epistle to the Corinthians Saint Paul says: '*Therefore I want you to understand that nobody speaking by the Spirit of God ever says "Let Jesus be cursed!" And nobody can say "Jesus is Lord" except by the Holy Spirit.*'[163] The words Holy Spirit and Spirit are synonymous. What exactly the words mean: '*...to say Lord under the influence of the Holy Spirit,*' is far from clear. Thousands of hypocrites, numerous heretics and sometimes even demons, overcome by the force of this name, have uttered this phrase. Surely, nobody would seriously claim that when all these people spoke the word 'Lord Jesus' they were filled with the Holy Spirit. But they would not be able truly to say '*Lord Jesus*' because only those who serve the word of God can truly say that Jesus is their Lord. This is true of the just. On the other hand, by their corrupt ways sinners make a blasphemy of the word of God, and their works cry out: '*anathema to Jesus.*'

"But those who are born of God do not sin but bear the divine spark in their hearts, they turn away from sin: and by their conduct they proclaim: Our

104

Father who art in heaven. The Holy Spirit Himself joins with their spirit in order to certify that they are sons of God; His heirs and joint heirs with Christ. They suffer with Him so that they may also be glorified with Him.[164]

"In accordance with their conduct these children of God do not say Abba, Father, half-heartedly. With all the purity of their heart, which is the source of right action, they truly believe in order to be justified, and accordingly, *they confess with the mouth, and so they are saved.*'[165]

The Saints are the images of the Son

"Therefore all their actions, all their words, and all their thoughts that the Word of God shapes in His image are a reflection of the invisible God and creator *who makes His sun rise on the evil and on the good, and sends rain on the righteous and on the unrighteous.*'[166] Therefore they are bearers of the celestial Word which is in itself the image of God.

"In this way, then, they are the image of the Image, the Son being the Image, and from then on they reflect His filiation not merely by external resemblance but by a deep assimilation. They are transformed by a spiritual renewal and on a very intimate plane they come to resemble He who is made manifest in the body of glory."

Sinners are the children of the Devil

"If, as we have seen, this is a description of those who truly say: *'Our Father who art in heaven,'* it should be evident that *'he who commits sins is a child of the devil,'* as Saint John says in his epistle, *'for the devil has been sinning from the beginning.'*[167] The spark of God which dwells in the renewed soul has an immunizing effect on those who reflect the image of his Son; but the seed of Satan infests those who commit sin and his presence prevents the necessary spiritual correction. Because the Son became manifest to destroy the works of the devil, the presence of the Word of God in our souls is capable of destroying in us the works of the devil, of extracting the infamous seed planted in us, and so making us children of God."

Becoming Divine

"Let us not imagine that we have only learned the formulation of a prayer to be said at fixed moments. If we truly understand what we have learned of the imperative *'we must pray without ceasing,'* our whole life will be an uninterrupted prayer that will enable us to proclaim: *'Our Father who art in heaven!'* Our city will no longer be on earth, but in heaven which is the throne of God, because the Kingdom of God will have been installed in all those who bear the image of the divine Word, and therefore they will have become divine."

NOTES

[152] Excerpts from *De Oratione*, ('On prayer', Migne, Greek Patrology, II, 485-549.) French Translation in A.G.Hammam, *Le Pater Explique par les Peres,* (Paris, Editions franciscaines, 1952,) pp 50-54.

[153] Paraphrase of Deuteronomy 32:18.

[154] Deuteronomy 32:6.

[155] Based on Deuteronomy 32:19-20.

[156] Isaiah 1:2.

[157] Malachi 1:6.

[158] Galatians 4:1-2.

[159] Romans 8:15.

[160] John 1:12

[161] An unusual translation of 1 John 3:9.

[162] Luke 11:1.

[163] I Corinthians 12:3.

[164] See Romans 8:16-17.

[165] Romans 10:10.

[166] Matthew 5:45.

[167] 1 John 3:8.

CHAPTER NINETEEN

The passage from Origen that we quoted in the previous chapter led us into the depth of the Lord's prayer.

In his turn, Saint Cyprien also analyzed each section of the Lord's prayer. Here we will quote some essential parts of his brief commentary.

It is interesting to note that right from the beginning he emphasises the communal and ecclesiastical character of this prayer. This was his main preoccupation. We must not forget that, after Saint Paul, Saint Cyprien was the fiercest advocate of the principle of the Church as community, communion with God as well as communion between men: a co-operative unity.

Saint Cyprien writes: [168]

"Let our Prayer be public and communal"

"And first, the Master of peace and unity did not want us to pray alone and individually, so that he who prays will not pray for himself alone. We do not say: 'My Father who art in heaven,' nor: 'Give me my daily bread.' And none of us prays only for himself that God cancels his debt; or that He exempts only him from temptation and He delivers him alone from Evil.

"Our prayer is public and communal, so when we pray we do not pray for one person alone but for a whole people, because with the whole people we are one. The God of peace and the master of harmony who teaches unity wanted each of us to pray for all, just as He carried all of us as one in Himself.

"The three youths in the furnace followed this law of prayer; they were united in prayer and become a single chorus. The scripture urges us to do so and teaches us how to pray; it gives us an example to imitate in order to follow its path. *'Thus these three in a single voice sang and thanked God ...'* [169]

"They spoke in a single voice although Christ had not yet taught them to pray. Their request was strong and effective because a calm, simple and spiritual prayer impresses God: *'All these, it is said, constantly devoted themselves to prayer, as did certain women, including Mary the mother of Jesus, as well as his brothers.'* [170]

They persevered in prayer as of one heart, which testifies to their great ardour and their unity. Because God, who gathers in his house the single hearted, admits in his divine and eternal quarters only those who pray in communion, each together with all the others."

"How generous and marvelous is the richness of the Lord's prayer! This richness is gathered together into few words, but it has a boundless spiritual density, so that no part is missing from this summary of the heavenly doctrine that forms our prayer. It is said: '*Pray in this way: Our Father who art in heaven.*'

"The new man, who is born anew and returned to his God by His grace, first says: 'Father,' because he has become a 'son.' '*He came to His own, and His own people did not accept Him. But to all who received Him, who believed in His name, he gave power to become children of God.*'[171] He who believes in His name and who has become a son of God must start by giving thanks and openly declare that he is a son of God. And when he calls God in heaven his 'Father,' by this he states that he renounces his carnal and earthly father, the father of his first birth, in order to know only one father, the one who is in heaven. Indeed, it is written: '*Who said of his father and mother "I regard them not...he ignored his kin and did not acknowledge his children. For they observed your word and kept your covenant.*'[172]

"In the gospel our Lord also asks us to refrain from calling anybody on earth 'our father.' To the disciple who speaks of his deceased father He says: '*Let the dead bury the dead.*'[173] The disciple spoke of a father who was dead, while the father of those who believe is alive."

God is the Father of those who believe and have been born again by Him

"It is not enough, dear brethren, to become aware that we are calling the Father who is in heaven, so we add: 'Our Father,' that is, Father of those who believe, of those who have been sanctified by Him, and have been born anew by the spiritual grace: they have begun to be sons of God.

"These words are also a condemnation and criticism of the Jews. In their lack of faith they despised the Christ who had been announced to them by the prophets, and sent to them first of all, and more, they put him to death cruelly. They can no longer call God their Father, because the Lord said to their confusion: '*You are from your father the devil, and you choose to do your father's desires. He was a murderer from the beginning and does not stand in the truth, because there is no truth in him.*'[174]

"*And through the prophet Isaiah, God shouted in indignation:*
I reared children and I have brought them up,
but they have rebelled against me.
The ox knows its owner,
and the donkey its master's crib;
but Israel does not know me,

and my people do not understand.
Ah, sinful nation, a people laden with iniquity,
offspring who do evil,
children who deal corruptly,
who have forsaken the Lord,
who have despised the Holy One in Israel,
who are utterly estranged. " [175]

"To blame them, Christians say in prayer: *Our Father;* in truth he has become our father and has stopped being father to the Jews when they abandoned Him. The treacherous people cannot be sons; but those whose sins were forgiven merit this title and have been promised eternity according to the word of the Lord; '*Everyone who commits sin is a slave to sin.*' [176] The slave does not remain forever in the house, but the son lives there forever."

If God is Father, we must behave like sons

"How great is the Lord's mercy, how great is his goodness and kindness that he allows us to pray in the presence of God, even to the ultimate favour of calling Him Father; and since Christ is the Son of God, so it is with us who are also called sons. Nobody among us would have dared to use this word in our prayer: it was the Lord Himself who encouraged us to do so.

"But we must remember, beloved brothers, that when we call God *our Father*, we must behave like sons of God. If we delight in having God for Father, then He must also find delight in us. We must be like temples of God, a place in which men can encounter His presence. Our conduct must not betray the Spirit; we have begun to become heavenly and spiritual, so now we must think and do only what is heavenly and spiritual. The Lord Himself said: '*For those who honour me I will honour, and those who despise me will be treated with contempt.*' [177] The apostle says in his epistle: '*You are not your own, for you were brought with a price; therefore glorify God in your body.*' [178]

Let us pray that holiness will dwell in us

"After this, we say: '*Hallowed be thy name.*' Not that we wish that God should be sanctified by our prayers, but rather we ask of Him that His name should be sanctified in us. For who could sanctify God when it is He Himself who sanctifies? But when we hear this word: '*You shall be holy to me; for I the Lord am holy,*' [179] we ask that, because we have been sanctified by baptism, we will persevere in what we have begun to be. And we must ask for this every day. It is imperative that we sanctify ourselves every day, because we sin daily;

we must cleanse ourselves of our sins by step by step sanctification without ceasing. These aspects of the sanctification that we owe to the divine compassion are best expressed by these words of the apostle: '*Fornicators, idolators, adulterers, male prostitutes, sodomites, thieves, greedy, drunkards, revilers, robbers — none of these will inherit the kingdom of God. And this is what you used to be. But you were washed, you were sanctified, you were justified in the name of the Lord Jesus Christ and in the Spirit of Our God.*'[180]

"He thus declares us sanctified in the name of our Lord Jesus Christ and in the spirit of our God. We therefore turn to prayer so that this sanctity can remain in us. Let us remember that our Lord and Judge asked the man whom He had just healed and made alive again '*to sin no more, so that nothing worse would happen to him;*'[181] this is why, for our part, we pray unceasingly, why we pray night and day in order that, with the help of God, we might be able to retain the sanctity and life which we owe to the divine grace."

We ask that the kingdom should come, as God has promised us

"'*Thy Kingdom come,*'that is how the prayer continues. We now ask that the Kingdom be made manifest to us in the same way that we wished His name to be made holy in us. Is it possible that God might not rule? When can something begin which has always existed and can never end? We pray for the coming of the Kingdom that has been promised, bought for us by the blood and the Passion of Christ. Before, we were slaves, now we ask that we might reign under the sovereignty of Christ. He Himself promised it to us, when He said: '*Come, ye blessed of my Father, inherit the kingdom prepared for you from the foundation of the world.*'[182]

"It is even possible, dear brethren, that the Kingdom of God refers to Christ in person, Him that we call on every day in our devotions and whose coming we wish to hasten by our attentions. Just as He is our resurrection — for in Him we are restored to life — he can also be the Kingdom of God, for it is also in him that we will rule.

"With good reason we ask for the Kingdom of God, that is, for the rule of heaven, which includes within it that of earth. But the one who challenged the common thinking of the world is above honours and kingdoms. That is why he who has given himself to God and to Christ does not yearn for the rule of earth, but of heaven.

"We have an unceasing need to pray, so that we will not lose the kingdom of heaven, as happened to the Jews who were promised the kingdom but lost it, according to the Lord's words: '*Many will come from the East and West, and will sit down with Abraham, and Isaac, and Jacob, in the kingdom of heaven, but the children of the Kingdom shall be cast out into outer darkness: there shall be*

110

weeping and gnashing of teeth.'[183] By these words He shows that the Jews were heirs of the Kingdom as long as they remained sons of God. When the paternity of God ended, the kingdom also came to an end. That is why we Christians, who call God *Our Father*, also pray that His Kingdom come within us."

We pray that Your will be done within us

"And we add: '*Thy will be done on earth as it is in heaven.*' This is not so that God may do as He wishes, but so that we may do what He wishes. For who can restrain God from doing what He wants? But we are opposed by the devil, who prevents our accepting the will of God both within ourselves and externally. This is why we ask that His will be done within us; but for this to occur we need His help. Nobody is strong enough in his own resources, but his strength resides in the goodness and mercy of God.

"The Lord himself showed the weakness He had assumed, when he said: '*My Father, if it is possible, let this cup pass from me.*'[184] And to show His disciples that it was not His own will that prevailed, but that of God, he added: '*Yet not my will but yours be done.*'[185] Elsewhere He is more specific: '*For I came down from heaven, not to do my own will, but the will of him that sent me.*'[186]

"If the Son Himself endorsed the necessity to do the will of God, how much more important is it that the servant do the will of the Lord, as is expressed in the *Epistle of John: 'Love not the world, neither the things that are in the world. If any man love the world, the love of the Father is not in him. For all that is in the world — the lust of the flesh, and the lust of the eyes, and the pride of life — is not of the Father, but is of the world. And the world passeth away, and the lust thereof: but he that doeth the will of God abideth forever.*'[187] Those who wish to live forever must do the will of God, who is eternal."

Christ did and taught the will of God

"The will of God is what Christ did and taught. Humility in conduct; firmness in faith; modesty in speech; justice in judgements; kindness in almsgiving; discipline in human morality; acting without prejudice; dignity and understanding when we are its victims; keeping the peace with our brothers; loving God with all our heart; to love Him because He is Father, and to fear Him because He is God; to prefer nothing above Christ, as He has preferred us above all; to bind ourselves unconditionally to His spirit of charity, but to take up our cross with courage and confidence; when the time comes to enter the battle in His name or in His honour; to demonstrate confidence in difficulties so as to remain strong in the struggle; patience in death in order to earn our crown. All of this is a clear sign of our will to be co-heir of Christ, to act according to the law of God, to do the will of God."

We pray that the will of God be done on earth
as it is in heaven,
that is to say: in our soul and in our body

"We ask that the will of God be done in heaven and on earth, because both of these contribute to our salvation. The body is from the earth and the soul from heaven, therefore we are heaven and earth. And we pray that in both, meaning in both our body and our soul, the will of God be done. Now there is a conflict between the flesh and the soul and every day there is a continuous struggle between the two. We do not do what we want: the soul seeks what is from heaven and from God, and the flesh seeks what is from earth and from the world. Thus we ask fervently that the help of God should impose harmony between the two, that the will of God should be done in the soul and in the body, and that the soul that God has made anew should be saved.

"This is what Saint Paul tells us very clearly: *'For what the flesh desires is opposed to the spirit, and what the spirit desires is opposed to the flesh; for these are opposed to each other, to prevent you from doing what you want. But if you are led by the spirit, you are not subject to the law. Now the works of the flesh are obvious: fornication, impurity, licentiousness, idolatory, sorcery, enmities, strife, jealousy, anger, quarrels, dissensions, factions, envy, drunkenness, carousing, and things like these. I am warning you, as I warned you before: those who do such things will not inherit the kingdom of God. By contrast, the fruit of the spirit is love, joy, peace, patience, kindness, generosity, faithfulness, gentleness and self-control.'* [188]

"This is why each day, even at each moment, we ask in our prayers that the will of God be done in heaven as on earth, because the will of God is that the things of the earth must give precedence to the things of heaven, that the share of the spirit and of God be the winner."

Another explanation of the same request

"Dear brethren, these words can also mean something else: as you know, our Lord urges us to love our enemies and to pray for those who persecute us. Thus we must pray for those who are still of this world and not of heaven, we must pray that they also accomplish the will of God that Christ accepted so perfectly for the salvation of humanity.

"Christ calls his disciples not earth, but 'salt of the earth,' and the Apostle says that the first man was extracted from the dust of the earth, and the second from heaven; we must come to resemble our heavenly Father who makes the sun rise on the pious and the impious, who bestows rain on the just and the unjust; for this reason, Christ makes us pray for the salvation of all men. In heaven, that is, the heaven within us, through faith, the will of God imposes itself in us and we are becoming divine; in the same way on earth, that is, in non-believers, we ask that the will of God be done: we also ask that those still in their first birth and still earthly become divine by a new birth through water and the Spirit."

NOTES

[168] De oratione dominca, (On the Lord's prayer, Migne, *Latin Patrology*, 4,521-538. The subtitles are taken from that work.)

[169] Attributed to Daniel but not found.

[170] Acts 1:14.

[171] John 1:11-12.

[172] Deuteronomy 33:9.

[173] Matthew 8:22.

[174] John 8:44.

[175] Isaiah 1:2-4.

[176] John 8:34.

[177] I Samuel 2:30.

[178] I Corinthians 6:19-20.

[179] Leviticus 20:26.

[180] I Corinthians 6:9-11.

[181] John 5:14.

[182] Matthew 25:34.

[183] Matthew 8:11-12.

[184] Matthew 26:39.

[185] Luke 22:42.

[186] John 6:38.

[187] I John 2:15-17.

[188] Paraphrased from Galatians 5:17-23.

CHAPTER TWENTY

COMMENTARY OF
SAINT CYPRIEN OF CARTHAGE
(Continued)
We ask for our bread, that is Christ;
so that we take leave neither of His blessing,
nor of His body

"As we continue, we say: *'Give us our daily bread.'*[189] These words may be taken in their spiritual or their literal meaning: in their providential design both meanings are made to contribute to our salvation.

"Our bread of life is Christ, and this bread does not belong to everybody, but it belongs to us. As we say *"Our Father"* because He is the Father of those who have faith, in the same way we call Christ our bread because He is the bread of those who constitute His body. To obtain this bread we pray each day: as we are in Christ and receive the host each day as nourishment for our salvation, we assume that we would not, because of a more serious sin, be deprived of holy communion. This would deprive us of the heavenly bread, as well as severing us from the body of Christ, as he warns us.

"He says: *'He who eats this bread will live eternally,'* in order to confirm that those who extend their hand toward His Body and receive the Host in communion may live; on the other hand we must ask with fear that those who voluntarily separate themselves from the Body of Christ may not exclude themselves from salvation. Our Lord warned us: *'Verily I tell you, unless you eat the flesh of the Son of Man and drink His blood, you have no life in you.'*[190] Therefore each day we ask to receive our bread, that is, Christ; to continue to live in Christ, and we also ask not to be separated from grace and His Body."

We must ask for our food each day,
not at long intervals

"It is also possible to understand this request in the following way: we have renounced the world; with the help of faith we have rejected its opulence and its seductions; we simply ask for the food we need, for as the Lord said: *'So therefore, none of you can become my disciple if you do not give up all your possessions.'*[191] He who is beginning to be a disciple of Christ and gives up everything, according to the word of the Lord, must ask for his daily nourishment but must not be concerned for the very long term. For again the

Lord said: *'Do not worry about tomorrow, for tomorrow will bring worries of its own. Today's trouble is enough for today.'* [192] The disciple justly asks his food for today because it is forbidden for him to worry about tomorrow. Therefore, it is not logical that those who ask for the early coming of the kingdom of God should want to prolong their stay in this world. The apostle warns us of this in order to train, strengthen and affirm our faith and our hope. *'For as we brought nothing into the world, so we can take nothing out of it; but if we have food and clothing we should be content with these. But those who want to be rich fall into temptation and are trapped by many senseless and harmful desires that plunge people into ruin and destruction.'* [193]

Christ teaches us that riches are more than contemptible: they are dangerous

"Christ teaches us that riches are more than contemptible: they are dangerous, they contain the root of all evil whose seducing and misleading appearances lead the human spirit astray. To the foolishness of the rich man who indulged in the opulence of the world and boasted about his overwhelming harvest God replied: *'You fool! This very night your life is being demanded of you. And the things you have collected, whose will they be?'* [194]

"This fool boasted about his harvest when that same night he was to die. He was thinking about his unlimited supplies while life had already abandoned him. On the other hand, the Lord declares that he who is perfect sells all that he has, gives it to the poor, and builds himself treasure in heaven.

"Moreover he adds that we can follow his traces and imitate his glorious Passion if we make ourselves free and liberate ourselves from the worry of everyday affairs, if also, in ridding ourselves of our belongings, we offer them to God as a sign of our offering of ourselves."

To him who possesses God, nothing is lacking if he does not fail God

"Daily bread cannot be lacking to the just, because it is written: *'The Lord does not let the righteous go hungry.'* [195] And elsewhere: *'I was young and I grew old; I have never seen one of the just abandoned nor his descendants look for bread.'* [196] Thus the Lord promises: *'Therefore do not worry saying, What shall we eat? or What will we drink? or What will we wear? For it is the gentiles who strive for all these things; and indeed your heavenly Father knows that you need all these things. But strive first for the kingdom of God and His righteousness, and all these things will be given you as well.'* [197]

"To those who are seeking the Kingdom and the justice of God He promises to give everything else. In truth everything belongs to God; he who possesses God lacks nothing if he himself does not fail God. In this way, when Daniel was thrown in the lions' den on the king's orders he received his meal from God; and this man of God began eating among the famished wild beasts who spared him.[198] Elijah was also given food during his journey and also while he was being persecuted, when in solitary confinement, ravens and other birds came to him and brought him food.[199] Alas, what detestable cruelty we find in humans: animals show concern, birds bring food, but men erect obstacles and exercise their cruelty."

After asking for our food,
we ask that our sins be forgiven, so that nobody
is in error about his innocence

"After that we pray for our sins. *'And forgive us our trespasses as we forgive those who have trespassed against us.'* After our food we ask that our sins be forgiven. He who is fed by God must live in God and be preoccupied not only with the present temporal life but also with the eternal. It is possible for him to reach it if his sins are forgiven. The Lord calls those sins *'debts'*, according to the Gospel: *'I forgave you all that debt because thou desiredst me.'*[200]

"Indeed it was necessary, wise, and salutary for the Lord to remind us that we are sinners by asking us to pray for our sins. In this way as we resort to God's indulgence we recall the state of our conscience. In order that nobody regards himself complacently as if he were innocent, nor loses himself in this vanity, when he is asked each day to pray for his sins, he is reminded that he sins each day.

"John also warns us in his epistle: *'If we say that we have no sin, we deceive ourselves, and the truth is not in us. If we confess our sins, he who is faithful and just will forgive us our sins and cleanse us from all unrighteousness.'*[201] In his epistle he combines two things: we must pray for our sins, and in this prayer we must ask to be forgiven. He affirms that the Lord is faithful to pardon our sins according to His promise. Because He who teaches us to pray for our debts and our sins, at the same time promises a fatherly blessing and forgiveness."

By which rule are sins forgiven?

"The Lord specifies the conditions for his pardon: He forces us to remit the debts of our debtors to us in the same way that we ask that our sins be remitted. We cannot ask for the remission of our sins unless we act the same way towards our own debtors. Elsewhere He says: *'For with the judgment you make you will be judged, and the measure you give will be the measure you get.*'[202]

"The servant had been cleared of his debts by the master, but he refused to do the same towards one of his companions and he was therefore put in jail. He refused to pardon his companion, and he loses the pardon given him by the master.[203] In this instruction Christ teaches this truth in a very harsh way: *'And when ye stand praying, forgive, if you have aught against any; that your Father also which is in heaven may forgive you your trespasses.'*[204]

"You will therefore have no excuse on judgment day when you will be judged according to your own behaviour: you will go through exactly what you had others go through. God commands us to keep peace and harmony in his house and to live according to the law of the new birth; now that we have become sons of God we must be the guardians of the peace of God. To the unity of the Spirit must correspond the unity of souls and hearts. God does not accept the sacrifice of those who are causes of disunity, He sends them away from the altar so that they may make peace with their brothers: God wants to be pacified with prayers of peace. The most beautiful offering to God is our own peace, our own harmony, the unity of all the faithful in the Father, the Son and the Holy Spirit."

God accepts only the prayer of the peaceful

"During the times of the early sacrifices offered by Cain and Abel,[205] God did not consider the offering but the hearts: the gifts were acceptable if the hearts were. Abel, the just and peaceful, who offers his sacrifice with a pure soul, shows everyone how to present himself in the act of sacrifice, that is, in fear of God, with a simple heart and a sense of justice, harmony, and peace.

"In offering the sacrifice to God with such an attitude, he had the honour of himself becoming a precious offering and the first man called to the confession of martyrdom. He was foreshadowing the passion of the Lord by the glory of his blood, because in him dwelt the justice and peace of the Lord. Such beings are entitled to the crown, such beings, on Judgement day, will be judges alongside Christ.

"The dissidents, on the other hand, those who do not live in peace with their brothers, are condemned by the apostle and by the Bible; even if they were willing to be killed in the name of Christ they would remain guilty of having created disharmony among their brothers, for it is written: *'All who hate a brother or a sister are murderers, and you know that murderers do not have eternal life abiding in them.'*[206]

"He who prefers to imitate Judas rather than Christ cannot be with Christ. How terrible is this crime that even the baptism of blood cannot cleanse it! How severe is this accusation that even martyrdom cannot remove it!"

The enemy can do nothing against us
unless God has given permission

"The Lord insists on another request: *'Do not bear to see us tested by adversity.'*[207] By these words it seems the enemy can do nothing against us unless God has given permission. Therefore, our fear, our affection, and our attention must always be turned towards God, because in our numerous temptations the power of the Devil depends on the power of God. This the Scriptures prove when they say: *'Nebuchadnezzer of Babylon came up to Jerusalem and the city was besieged and the Lord delivered it into his hands.'*[208]

"According to the scriptures the devil is given this power against us because of our sins:

'Who gave up Jacob to the spoiler
and Israel to the robbers?
Was it not the Lord,
against whom they have sinned
in whose ways they would not walk
and whose law they would not obey?
So He poured upon Israel the heat of his anger.[209]

"And in connection with Solomon, who was sinning and deviating from the Lord's way, it is said: *'And the Lord raised Satan against him.'*"[210]

This power is granted either for our punishment or for our glory.
This request centres us on our weakness.

"God can give power to the devil in two ways: for our punishment when we have sinned, or for our glory if we are exposed to temptation. We saw that this was the case with Job: *'Very well, all that he has is in your power; only do not stretch out your hand against him!'*[211]

"In the Bible the Lord says: *'You would have no power over me unless it had been given you from above.'*[212] Therefore, when we pray not to be tempted we remember our weakness so that nobody thinks of himself as invulnerable, nobody thinks himself as better than he is, nobody gives himself credit for his faithfulness or his passion,[213] when the Lord Himself teaches humility as he says: *'Keep awake and pray that you may not come into the time of trial; the spirit indeed is willing, but the flesh is weak.'*[214] If we first show true humility, we will give everything we ask for back to God with fear and reverence, we can be assured then that His kindness will grant what we request."

118

The last request concerns everything
that the enemy is plotting against us

"After this our prayer ends with a conclusion that summarizes all the other requests. In the end we say: '*But deliver us from Evil.*' With these words we refer to what the enemy can muster against us, but we can rest assured that we have a powerful ally if God delivers us, if He helps those who implore Him. Thus when we say: '*Deliver us from Evil,*' there is nothing more to request: we have asked for the protection of God against the Devil. Having said this prayer we have become strong against all the schemes of the devil and the world. Who can fear the world if God is his protector in this world?"

NOTES

[189] As with the other Latin Fathers, Saint Cyprien speaks of 'daily bread,' while the Greek Fathers speak of 'Superessential' *(epiousion)* bread, or in an ancient Latin translation, 'supersubstantial'. But this changes nothing of the spiritual commentary. See the meticulous analysis by Origen of this term *epiousios* in his commentary on the Lord's Prayer.

[190] John 6:53.

[191] Luke 14:33.

[192] Matthew 6:34. Definitely a paraphrase to meet the needs of contemporary people.

[193] Again paraphrased from 1 Timothy 6:7-10.

[194] Luke 12:20.

[195] Proverbs 10:3.

[196] Psalms 37:25.

[197] Matthew 6:31-33.

[198] See Daniel 6:17-24.

[199] 1 Kings 17:4-6 and 19:5-8.

[200] Matthew 18:32.

[201] 1 John 1:8-9.

[202] Matthew 7:2.

[203] Matthew 18:23-25.

[204] Mark 11:25.

[205] Based on the story of Cain and Abel; See Genesis 4:1-16.

[206] 1 John 3:15.

[207] Saint Cyprian uses this phrase: '*to be led into temptation*' (see p.99.)

[208] Seems to be an unusual rendering from 2 Kings 24:10.

[209] Isaiah 42:24.

[210] Saint Cyprian interprets the phrase from the first book of Kings: '*The Lord raised up an adversary against Solomon*'[211] referring to a prince of Edom (see also 11:23) as meaning the Adversary or Satan.

[212] Paraphrased from Job 1:12.

[213] John 19:11.

[214] In the classical sense of being 'passive' to events. (Ed.)

CHAPTER TWENTY-ONE

COMMENTARY OF SAINT CYRIL OF JERUSALEM
(Extracts.)

In his fifth mystical catechism, Saint Cyril of Jerusalem also comments on the Lord's prayer: [215] *"Afterwards, we say the prayer that the Lord taught to His disciples; with a pure heart we call God our Father, and we say: 'Our Father who art in Heaven.'* God's love for men is infinite. To those who had erred from Him and had thrown themselves in the worst of calamities He gives His full pardon for their wrongdoing; this pardon is of such immense import that it allows them to say to Him: *'Father! Our Father who art in Heaven.'*

"Heaven also means all those who bear in themselves the celestial image; God resides in them because He has established His abode in them.

"*'Hallowed be thy Name.'* The Name of God is sanctified by nature, whether we realize it or not. But our sins have defiled it, as it is written; '*Because of you my Name is blasphemed continually each day.'*[216]

"Thus we ask that His Name be sanctified in us; not that it has to become holy as if it had not always been so, but rather because of the fact that we strive that we should become sanctified and live as saints of God.

"*'Thy Kingdom come.'* Only a pure heart can say with confidence '*Thy Kingdom come.'* One must have followed Paul's teachings so as to say: '*Therefore do not let sin exercise dominion in your mortal bodies...'*[217] Only he who keeps himself pure in his actions, his thoughts, and his words, can say to God: '*Thy Kingdom come.'*

"*'Thy will be done in heaven as it is done on earth.'* The holy angels of God do the will of God. Indeed, in Psalms David says: '*Bless the Lord, O you his angels, you mighty ones who do his bidding.'*[218] When you pray in this way, you say, essentially: '*As the angels in heaven do your will, Lord, let it be the same on earth: let Thy will be done in me.'*

"*'Give us today the bread necessary for our subsistence.'*[219] It is not ordinary bread that is needed for our nourishment, but holy bread: it must nourish the substance of the soul. This kind of bread does not go through digestion and decomposition, rather it expands throughout your being for the health of your soul and your body. Here 'today' means every day; this is how Paul expresses his thought when he says: '*While it is called today.'*[220]

"*'Forgive us our trespasses as we forgive those who trespass against us.'* We have committed numerous sins. We sin in thought, in speech, and in a great number of our actions which are truly reprehensible. '*If we say that we have no sin, we deceive ourselves.'*[221] We make a contract with God when we ask him to forgive our sins as we forgive those who have sinned against us. Let us make sure that we really think about what it is that we receive and at what cost. Let us not wait and refuse to forgive others. Those wrongs of which we are victims are minimal, insignificant and without much consequence; those, on the contrary, that we have committed against God are important and it is only through the divine charity that we can be pardoned. So make sure that you are not refused the pardon of your very serious sins committed against God because you have refused to pardon small offenses.

"*Lord, do not lead us into temptation.*' Must we think that the Lord expects us to pray that we should never be tried at all? It is said in the Scriptures: *'He who has never been tried has not proved himself.*'

"And elsewhere: '*Whenever you face trial of any kind, consider it nothing but joy.*'[222]

"But would not 'to be tried' in our text mean 'to be overwhelmed by trials?'

"Indeed, it may seem that this trial is a very strong current that is most difficult to cross. Those who are not overwhelmed by the trial are the only ones who can overcome it; they are, so to speak, good swimmers who are not washed away by the current. The others, as they try, drop to the bottom.

"Let us take Judas, for instance; he was tempted by greed. He could not, in a way, swim across this temptation; he was lost, body and soul. Peter, on the other hand, was tempted to give up; but in the end he avoided disaster, managed to reach the other shore and was rescued. In another text the choir of saints who had remained pure sings its gratitude:

"*For you, O God have tested us;*
you have tried us as silver is tried
You have brought us to the net;
You laid burdens over our backs;
You let people ride over our heads;
we went through fire and water;
yet You have brought us out to a spacious place."[223]

"Take good notice of the joy they experienced because they made the crossing without perishing. '*And you have brought us out*' it is said, '*to a spacious place.*' Spacious place here means: to come out of the test.

"'*But deliver us from Evil.*' If '*do not lead us into temptation.*' meant to remove all trials, Jesus would not have added '*But deliver us from Evil.*' Evil is the devil, and we ask to be delivered from him.

"And at the end of this prayer you say: '*Amen.*' This means that you confirm everything that is contained in this prayer."

122

NOTES

215 Mark 14:38.

216 Mystical Catechism (Migne, *Greek Patrology* 33, 11117-1124). French trans. in Le Pater explique par les peres (ibid. pp. 106-109).

217 Isaiah 52:5 Based on the French Bible text which is very different from the English.

218 Romans 6:12.

219 Psalms 103:20.

221 Hebrews 3:13.

222 1 John 1:8.

223 James 1:2.

CHAPTER TWENTY-TWO

*Prayer at the dawn of Christianity;
the Apostolic tradition*

Having considered the previous wonderful commentaries, let us now see how the faithful prayed at the dawn of Christianity. We will quote from two passages; one from the Apostolic Tradition and the other from the works of Origen.

The Apostolic Tradition[224] tells us of *"the time of prayer,"* which is very close to what we call now the large and small hours of liturgy.

Let us recall here the famous alphabetical Psalm 119 [225] in which the psalmist urges us to rise seven times a day, (that is, seven times during each 24 hours) to praise the Lord.

The Time of Prayer

"Let all the faithful, men and women, as soon as they come out of sleep in the morning, wash their hands and pray to God, and then go to their occupations.

"If, however, there is a sermon, one must give it priority, as we are convinced that God speaks through the words of the preacher. He who has thus prayed with his brothers is provided against the burden of the day. He who fears God must feel it a loss not to participate in the gathering, especially if he can read.

"When the preacher has arrived, all the faithful must hurry to the place of meeting where the homily will be given. There, the preacher will speak to each one. You will hear things about which you were not thinking, and you will profit from what the Spirit tells you from the mouth of the person who is speaking. In this way your faith will be strengthened by what you will hear. You will also be told how to live correctly in your home. Yes indeed, each one of you must remain firm in your habit of going to the gathering where the Holy Spirit brings His riches to you all. *'On days when there is no instruction let each of you bring home a holy book and read for the profit of your soul.'"*

Hours Of Prayer

"If you are at home, pray at the third hour [226] and praise God. If you are somewhere else at that time pray with all your heart, because it is at that hour that Christ was put to the cross. For this reason, the Law of the Old Testament ordered the shewbread to be offered at that hour — a sign of the Body and Blood of Christ — and to sacrifice a witless lamb which was a prefiguration of the perfect Lamb. Indeed, Christ is the shepherd, just as He is the bread that has come from heaven.

"You will pray in the same way at the sixth hour [227] while remembering Christ on the cross as the day had ended and darkness was everywhere. At that hour you will pray in a very forceful way to imitate He who prayed for the unbelieving Jews when the universe was in darkness.

"At the ninth hour,[228] extend your prayer and your praise to imitate the souls of the just who praise the God of truth, He who remembered His saints and sent the Word to bring them light. At that hour, with His chest open, shedding water and blood, he illuminated the dusk of that day until His dying. And by bringing together the return of light with His sleep, He gave an image of His resurrection.

"Pray also before you rest your body. Around the middle of the night, get up, wash your hands with water, and pray. If your wife is there, pray together. If she is not a Christian yet, go into another room and pray, then go back to sleep.

"Do not neglect this prayer. He who is married is not impure for that: '*One who has bathed does not need to wash, but is entirely clean.*'[229] While signing yourself with your humid breath, and in holding your saliva in your hand, your body is entirely clean, right down to your feet. Because the gift of the Spirit, and the rite of the lustral water which bursts out like a spring [230] and is received in a pure heart, have purified the faithful.

"We must then pray at that hour because the Ancients, from whom we take this tradition, have taught us that at that moment the whole of creation falls still to pray to the Lord. The stars, the trees and the water stop for a moment; and the whole choir of the angels unite with the souls of the just to sing the praises of God. It is thus very important that the faithful pray at that hour.

"The Lord Himself confirms this when He says: '*Here is the bridegroom! Go out to meet him.*'[231] And he concludes: '*Therefore stay awake, for you know neither the day nor the hour.*'[232]

"At cock-crow get up one more time and do the same. At the hour when the cock was crowing the sons of Israel adjured Christ whom we knew through faith; we are waiting for the day of the resurrection of the dead, in the hope of eternal light.

"Therefore, you who are faithful, if you behave that way and remember the mysteries while teaching each other and setting a good example for the catechumens, you will neither fall into temptation nor lose your souls, because you remember Christ unceasingly."

"In all circumstances make an effort to sign yourself in a noble way. This sign of the Passion is a well-tried defense against the Devil, as long as you do it in a spirit of faith and not in vain display, thus protecting yourself as with a shield. When the Enemy sees the inner force represented externally, which signifies our resemblance to the Word, he flees, not because you scare him but because of the Spirit which breathes in you. Moses sacrificed a lamb and sprinkled the threshold and the sides of the doors. In this way he signified the faith that we now have in the perfect Lamb. Let us sign our foreheads and our eyes with our hand in order to chase away the One that seeks our loss."

NOTES

224 Attributed to Saint Hypolyte of Rome, third century, (see other translation in Sources Chretiennes, no. 11 bis). The quotations reproduce paragraphs 41 and 42.

225 Psalm 119 in the numbering of the Hebrew psalm-book, 118 in the Latin (Vulgate) psalm-book. The present quotation refers to verse 164.

226 That is, at approximately 9 o'clock.

227 Noon.

228 Three o'clock in the afternoon.

229 John 13:10.

230 Reference to baptism.

231 Matthew 25:6.

232 Matthew 25:13

CHAPTER TWENTY-THREE

Prayer at the dawn of Christianity: Origen

Origen speaks of the value of prayer; of its transformative force. He teaches us that Christ and the angels pray with us. Then he shows us how to pray unceasingly, and comments on the content of the petition, on the act of meditation, and on the place of prayer.[233]

The fruits of prayer

"I believe that one who prays correctly according to his abilities receives numerous advantages from prayer. First, it is very important to set one's mind to prayer; through this preparation the faithful brings himself into the presence of God, he prepares himself to speak to Him, as to someone he sees, someone who is present. If it is true that certain images, certain memories of the past remain present in our mind to such a degree that they confuse our thoughts, how important is it to recognize the beneficial effects of the mind of God present in us when the faithful becomes conscious of this look which penetrates the innermost secret of his heart; and how important that the soul tries to please this heavenly witness who probes all his spirit, who sounds people's hearts.

"Even if we assume that the faithful who sets his soul to prayer does not profit in any other way, we should not underestimate the spiritual benefits of such an effort. If he makes a habit of it, how well he avoids sin and how much progress he makes towards virtue. Those who truly persevere in prayer know this well through experience. If the thought and memory of a great man is already enough to bring out the best in us and inhibit our tendency towards evil, in prayer how much more does the remembrance of God, the Father of the Universe, support those who perceive that He is present, those who speak to Him, those whom God sees and hears."

To accept everything without complaint

"It is evident that he who prays thus has no sooner finished praying than he hears the answer: '*Here I am.*' This is on condition that before praying he removed any difficulty concerning Providence; this is what is meant by these words: '*If you remove the yoke from among you, the pointing of the finger, the speaking of evil.*'[234]

"He who accepts everything that comes to him is free from any enslavement, he does not raise his hands to a God who orders what he wants for our formation. He does not even whisper secret thoughts which go undetected by other men. It is the characteristic of unworthy servants to complain; they complain against what comes to them without raising their voice, but with all the force of their soul, as if they wanted to hide the object of their complaints from providence and from the Lord of the universe.

"It is this, it seems to me, that the book of Job refers to: '*In all this Job did not sin with his lips.*'[235] In relation to earlier sufferings it is written: '*In all this Job did not sin or charge God with wrong-doing.*'[236] And on this subject we find in Deuteronomy: '*Be careful that you do not entertain a mean thought, thinking, the seventh year, the year of remission, is near.*'"[237]

He who prays in this way, participates in the prayer of the Word

"He who prays in this way receives all the graces, so that he becomes more able to unite with '*the Spirit which fills all the universe.*'[238] and who lives on earth and in heaven according to the word of the prophet: '*Do I not fill heaven and earth says the Lord.*'[239]

"Furthermore, by this purification which was mentioned earlier, he will participate in the prayer of the Word of God, who stands even among those who ignore Him, and who is absent from nobody's prayer. He prays to the Father in union with the faithful of whom he is the mediator. Indeed, the Son of God is the High Priest of our offerings and our advocate with the Father;[240] He prays for those who pray, He pleads for those who must defend themselves. But he refuses his fraternal assistance to those who do not pray through Him with perseverance; He does not make His own the cause of those who ignore His command: '*You must pray always and not lose heart.*'[241]

"Indeed it is written: '*he told them a parable about their need to pray always and not to lose heart: in a certain city there was a judge, etc.*'[242] And before that: '*And he said to them, "suppose one of you has a friend, and you go to him at midnight and say to him, 'Friend, lend me three loaves of bread; for a friend of mine has arrived and I have nothing to set before him, etc.*'"[243] And further on: '*I tell you, even though he will not get up and give him anything because he is his friend, at least because of his persistence he will get up and give him whatever he needs.*'"[244]

The angels and the saints pray for us

"The High Priest is not alone in uniting with the faithful who really pray, there are still the angels, who, the Scriptures say, rejoice in heaven for a single sinner who repents more than for the other ninety-nine who do not have to repent.[245]

"It is the same with the souls of the saints who have fallen asleep."

"The highest virtue, according to the divine word, is charity towards our neighbour; we must admit that the saints who are already dead practice this virtue towards those who struggle in this life, even more so than those who still have to experience human weakness and who manage to help those weaker than them. For: *'If one member suffers, all suffer together with them; if one member is honoured, all rejoice together with them.'* [246] That is realised by those who love their brothers. But it is also possible to apply, to the love which is exercised in the life beyond the present life, the word of the apostle: *'The preoccupation of all Churches! If one is weak, let me be weak, if someone falls, let fire devour me?* [247]

"Does not Christ himself say that He is ill in each of his saints who are ill, that He is in prison, that He is naked, that He is homeless, that He is thirsty? [248] Of those who have read the Bible, who does not know that Christ made all the suffering of believers His own?"

The gathering of the angels around Christ

"If the angels came to Jesus to serve Him [249] it must not be assumed that this ministering towards Jesus was limited to the short time of His stay on earth among men, and thus that He found Himself among the faithful, not: *'For whether is greater, he that sitteth at meat, or He that serveth?'*[250]

"We may wonder how many angels serve Jesus, who wishes to gather each and every son of Israel and those of the diaspora;[251] who saves those who fear Him and pray to Him? And in number how many more than the apostles work to extend the reach of the Church.[252] We read in the Revelation of Saint John that the angels are at the head of the Church.[253] It is thus no surprise that angels are seen ascending and descending around the Son of man, and that they become manifest to those who are illuminated by the light of knowledge."[254]

...and around those who pray

"At the time of prayer, the angels are informed by the person who prays of the needs that press on him, and they act according to their powers by the universal mandate they were entrusted with. Let me make a comparison to illustrate what I mean. Let us imagine a physician near a sick person who has prayed for her recovery.

129

"This physician knows how to cure a disease. We can be sure that he will give the right prescription to his patient, convinced that in this way he accomplishes the will of God, in himself answering the prayer of the patient.

"Or let us imagine a man who is blessed with a superabundance of earthly possessions; he is a charitable man who hears the petition of a destitute person who asks God for help. Here again it is certain that the rich man will help the poor person, acting as an agent of the divine will. Intentionally, God has come near, at the moment of prayer, to the one who has made the request and also to the one who is in a position to help; He has not let the latter remain insensible to the needs of the former.

"In such encounters it would surely be incorrect to assume that they came to be by chance only; the truth here is that God, who has counted all the hairs on the saints' heads,[255] has brought together the one who can help and the one who is waiting for him.

"In the same way we may think that the angels are near those who pray and help in the answer to their prayers because they are the intendants and helpers of God. Moreover, the angel assigned to each of us, even those who have a small place in the Church, unceasingly sees the Face of the Lord who is in heaven[256] and contemplates the divinity of our Creator. He prays with and sustains us according to His powers."

How to pray without ceasing

"In the same way that the work of virtue and the accomplishment of the commandments are part of prayer, he who joins prayer to necessary works and the works to prayer prays without ceasing. In this way only can we consider that the injunction to pray without ceasing is feasible. The essence of this injunction is to consider the totality of the life of the saint as a great prayer, of which what we usually call prayer is but a small portion. This latter type of prayer must be done three times a day, as in the case of Daniel, who prayed three times a day when he was threatened by danger.[257]

"Peter also went up to the roof to pray, around the sixth hour, when he saw coming down from heaven, a sort of large sheet lowered to the ground by its four corners.[258] This relates to the second of these three prayers, which David spoke of before him:

"O Lord, in the morning you hear my voice; In the morning I plead my case to you, and watch."

"The third prayer is expressed by these words; 'And the lifting up of my hands as an evening sacrifice.'[259]

"We do not even go through the night without praying, as David says: 'At midnight I rise to praise you because of your righteous ordinances.'[260]

"And from Paul, the Acts say: *'About midnight at Phillippi, Paul and Silas were praying and singing hymns to God, and the prisoners were listening to them.'*"[261]

What we must ask

"Now let us meditate on this word: *'Ask the important things and the small one will be given to you in addition; ask for the blessings of heaven and those of the earth will be given to you in addition.'*[262] Compared to the reality of the true and spiritual blessing, all the images and figures are weak and base. But the word of God urges us to imitate the prayer of the saints so that we can receive in reality what they received in images. It reminds us also that the celestial and important goods are signified by earthly and modest goods. As if He were saying: *'you want to be spiritual beings? In your prayers ask for the blessings of heaven, and once you have received them you will inherit the kingdom of heaven: once you have become strong you will receive even greater blessings. As for the usual earthly goods which you need for your daily sustenance, the Father also gives them to you as they become necessary.'*

Attitudes in prayer

"It seems to me that he who is about to pray must turn inwards and prepare himself somewhat in order to be more alert, more attentive to the context of the prayer. He must also disperse all anxieties and all affliction of the mind, and try to remember the immensity of God whom he approaches. He must keep in mind that it is baseness to stand before Him without concentration, without effort, and without due respect. Finally, he must remove all unnecessary thought.

"In coming to prayer one must, so to speak, present his soul before his hands, raise his spirit before his eyes, extricate his spirit from the world before rising to present it to the Lord of the universe. And finally, if he wishes God to forget the evil that he has committed against Him, against his neighbour, or against reason, he must rid himself of all resentment about offenses of which he has supposedly been victim.

"As the postures of the body are numerous, to express with our body the image of the dispositions of our soul during prayer, that position in which we extend our hands and raise our eyes towards heaven must have priority over all others. We say that we must act this way when there is no obstacle. But sometimes circumstances force us to pray in a sitting position when, for example, we have sore feet; or sometimes in bed because of a fever. For the same reason, if, for example, we are on a ship, or our occupations do not allow us to withdraw into privacy to do our prayer duty, it is permissible to do away with exterior dispositions.

"As for kneeling prayer, this is obligatory when we confess our sins before God, asking Him to heal and absolve them. This prayer is the symbol of the prostration and submission about which Paul spoke when he wrote: '*For this reason I bow my knees before the Father, from whom every family in heaven and on earth takes its name.*' [263] This kneeling is called spiritual because every creature adores God in the name of Jesus and humbles itself before Him. The apostle appears to refer to this when he says: '*So that at the name of Jesus every knee should bend, in heaven and on earth and under the earth.*'" [264]

The place of prayer

"As for the place, one must know that any place is appropriate for him who prays correctly. However, if one wants to do his prayers in greater quiet and less distraction he may choose a specific place in his home, if it is possible, a consecrated place, so to speak, and pray there.

"There is a particular grace and a certain utility in the place of prayer, by this I mean the place of gathering of the faithful. It is certain that the powers of the angels are a part of the gathering of the faithful and that the virtue of our Lord and Saviour is also present there. Also present are the spirits of the saints, and those, if I may add, of the dead who have preceded us, as well as those of the saints who are still living, although it is difficult to explain how.

"Here is what can be thought of the angels: '*The angel of the Lord encamps around those who fear Him, and delivers them.*'[265]

Jacob tells the truth not only when he speaks about himself, but also when he speaks about all those who serve God as he says '*The angel has redeemed me from all harm.*'[266] It is therefore possible to state: in the assembly of numerous brothers gathered for the glory of Christ, each one has his angel who surrounds those who fear God, and who stands near him whom he has the task of defending and protecting. In the assembly of saints, two Churches [267] are united: that of men and that of the angels.

"If indeed the angel Raphael can say of Tobit that he presented his prayer [268] to God, and later that of Sarah, who became his daughter-in-law, what then can we not say about the assembly of those who, united in one spirit, in one thought, constitute a single body in Christ?"

EPILOGUE

This book on the technique of prayer aims only at the opening of the soul, spirit, and will of man to the divine life. If one does more than read it, if he takes it to the stage of an experience, the results will be beneficial; and the reader of this instruction will personally profit and progress in the way which leads to health and sanctity of being.

For this there remains one indispensable condition:
to be faithful to the message of Christ.

NOTES

[233] In the remainder of his treatise on prayer.
[234] Isaiah 58:9.
[235] Job 2:10.
[236] Job 1:22.
[237] Deuteronomy 15:9.
[238] Wisdom 1:7.
[239] Jeremiah 23:24.
[240] See John 2:1.
[241] Luke 18:1.
[242] Based on Luke 18:1-7 quoted above.
[243] Luke 11:5-8.
[244] Luke 11:8.
[245] Luke 15:5.
[246] 1 Corinthians 12:26.
[247] This is the section of Luke which has just been quoted: 18:1 to 7.
[248] Possibly a confused reference to Revelation 22: 11.
[249] See Matthew 4:11.
[250] Luke 22:27.
[251] See Isaiah 27:12 and John 11:52.
[252] How many more than the apostles are the angels who do this work?
[253] Revelation 1:20 and chapters 2 and 3.
[254] John 1:51
[255] Matthew 10:30, Luke 12:7.
[256] Matthew 18:10.

[257] Daniel 6:10.

[258] Acts 10:9 and following

[259] Psalms 141:2.

[260] Psalms 119:62.

[261] Acts 16:25.

[262] This "word" does not correspond to any literal quotation from the Bible but summarizes the dominant theme of the parable of the "lillies of the field." (Matthew 6:25 and Luke 12:22-31).

[263] Ephesians 3:14-15.

[264] Philippians 2:10.

[265] Psalms 34:7.

[266] Genesis 48:16.

[267] Church in its etymological meaning of ECCLESIA, that is, ASSEMBLY.

[268] To clarify: Raphael presented Tobit's prayer to God. See Tobit 12:152-14.